Investing for Beginners - 2 Books in 1

Discover the Magic Strategies the Best Investors Use to Create Generational Wealth and Become Financially Independent!

By Warren Bell

ETF Investing Like for Market Wizardz!

Learn the Magic Strategies to Defeat Mr. Market Without Doing Stock Picking or Trading - Design Your Financial Success!

By Warren Bell

the reader will render any resulting actions solely under their purview. There are no scenarios in which the publisher or the original author of this work can be in any fashion deemed liable for any hardship or damages that may befall them after undertaking information described herein.

Additionally, the information in the following pages is intended only for informational purposes and should thus be thought of as universal. As befitting its nature, it is presented without assurance regarding its prolonged validity or interim quality. Trademarks that are mentioned are done without written consent and can in no way be considered an endorsement from the trademark holder.

Table of Contents

Introduction

Stocks have taken the world by storm once again after their recovery from the crash of March 2020. After a correction of more than 3 months, the most famous index, the S&P 500 surpassed its previous all time high.

A lot of people are now trying to improvise themselves as professional investors and are losing a lot of money, only helping those who actually know what they are doing accumulate an incredible amount of wealth that will lead to generational fortunes.

To join the club of the few investors that actually make it, you need the right strategies and the right mindset. Notice how we did not include a large initial capital. In fact, while having more money to trade with means having more fire power, it is not necessary to have thousands of dollars to accumulate stocks and build wealth.

In fact, when we started investing in stocks we only had a few hundreds to put into the market, but that sum yielded us thousands and thousands of dollars over the span of a few years.

In this book you are going to discover all the strategies that have allowed us to take investing skills to the next level and everything that helped us understand the stock market. If you diligently apply our advice, we are sure you are going to see amazing results in a relative short period of time, since this market is offering an amazing number of opportunities.

Please, stay away from all the shiny objects of the stock market. Just focus on a few stocks, study them deeply and then milk them like a cash cow. That is the real secret of market wizards!

To your success!

Chapter 1

Before Investing

If you are reading this book, you are interested in investing to generate wealth. However, there is one thing you need to do before even considering putting a dollar in the stock market. Since this book is dedicated to beginners, we feel it is important to spend the first chapter talking about an even more important topic: saving.

In fact, we believe that if you have an emergency fund of at least 6 months, you should focus on building that first before investing. Why? Because by having some cash set aside you will not have to disinvest in case of an emergency. You can easily calculate this number by multiplying your monthly income by 6. For instance, if you earn $5,000 a month, we advise you to set aside an emergency fund of 30,000$ before investing.

Let's take a look at some of the basics of saving money.

Everyone knows saving is a wise choice in the long run, but many of us still have a hard time doing it. To save money, it is not enough to spend less - and even this trick is not easy to put into practice. Smart savers also consider how to spend the money they have and how to maximize their income.

Pay yourself first

The easiest way to save money is to make sure you never get a chance to spend it. Establishing that part of your salary is deposited directly into a savings account or a pension fund allows you not to worry about how much money you should save each month; in practice, you save automatically and you can spend all the money you have left as you like. Over time, putting even a small portion of each salary into your savings can make a difference (especially when considering interest), so get started early to get the most benefit.

To establish an automatic deposit, talk to the payroll person at your job (or, if your company uses them, the payroll service). If you will provide the information of a deposit account other than the checking account where you receive the salary, you should be able to establish a direct deposit without problems.

If for some reason you cannot get an automatic deposit for each month (for example because you work as a freelancer or because you are paid in cash), you can decide how much money to manually deposit into a savings account each month and always follow your guidelines.

Avoid getting into debt

In some cases, getting into debt is essential. For example, only very rich people have enough money to pay for a house in a lump sum, but millions of people manage to buy real estate thanks to mortgages. In general, though, if you can avoid getting into debt, do it. In the long run, paying the money owed at the time of purchase is always a more advantageous solution than repaying a loan that accumulates interest over time.

If you can't help but take out a loan, try to pay the highest possible down payment. The greater the part of the purchase that you can deal with immediately, the sooner you pay off the debt and the lower the interest.

Even though everyone's financial situation is different, most banks recommend that debt amounts to around 10% of gross income and consider a solid situation to be 20%. 36% is considered to be the upper limit of the reasonable amount of debt one should have. We advise you to stay debt free as much as possible.

Have saving goals

It's much easier to save money if you have a goal to aim for. Set goals within your reach to motivate you to make the difficult financial decisions needed to save responsibly. It can take years or decades to achieve the most important results, such as buying a house or retiring. In these cases, it is important to check your progress on a regular basis. Only by taking a step back and observing the situation from afar you can understand how far you have come, and how much more you have to go.

More ambitious goals, such as retirement, can only be achieved after a long time. In the required period, the financial markets will change several times. You may want to research the future market trend before setting yourself a goal. For example, if you are at the beginning of your career, many finance experts argue that you should save around 60-85% of your annual income to maintain your lifestyle for each retirement year.

Establish a time window for your goals. Setting ambitious (but reasonable) time limits to reach your goals can be a great motivational boost. For example, imagine you want to own a house within two years from now. In this case, you will need to research the average price of houses in the area where you would like to live and start saving for the down payment on your new home (as a general rule, the down payments must represent 20% of the total cost of the home).

In our example, if the houses in the area you have chosen cost around $300,000, you will need to be able to save around $60,000 over two years. Depending on your income, this may not be a realistic goal.

Setting time limits is especially important for short-term goals. For example, if you have to repair your car, but you can't afford the cost of maintenance you should save the money you need for it as soon as possible, so as not to risk being left without a means of transport to get to the workplace. An ambitious but reasonable time limit can help you achieve this goal.

Keep a personal budget

It's easy to commit to ambitious savings goals, but if you don't have a way to keep track of your spending, it will be very difficult to succeed. To keep track of your financial progress, try to budget based on your salary at the beginning of each month. Allocating a portion of your income to all your major expenses ahead of time can help you avoid wasting money, especially if you split each paycheck right away as soon as you receive it.

Make a note of the different expenses. Staying on a budget is essential for anyone looking to save, but if you don't keep track of your expenses, it will be much more difficult to achieve your goals. Keeping track of what your monthly outgoings are can help you identify areas where you need to learn to contain yourself to stay within your budget. To do this, you need great attention to detail. While we should all take note of the most important expenses, such as rent and mortgage payments, the attention you should devote to smaller purchases depends on the severity of your financial situation.

It may be helpful to always carry a small notebook with you. Get in the habit of recording all expenses and keeping receipts. When you have the chance, write the amounts down in a larger notebook or an online spreadsheet. Note that there are many applications available for your phone today that can help you keep track of your expenses.

If you spend too much, don't be afraid to keep all your receipts. At the end of the month, divide them into categories, then count the total expenses. You may be amazed at how much money you waste on unnecessary purchases.

Check the amount of all payments several times. Always ask for a receipt when making a purchase in person and always print a copy of online purchases. Make sure you always pay the right price and don't get charged for things you don't want - you'd be surprised how often this happens.

Don't split your expenses just because it's convenient. If your meal costs a third of that of the friend you had lunch with at the restaurant, you shouldn't pay half the bill.
Consider downloading an app for your smartphone to help you calculate tips more accurately.

Start saving as soon as possible

Money stored in savings accounts accrue interest at fixed percentages. The longer your money stays in the account, the more interest you will earn. This is why it is advantageous to start saving as soon as possible. Even if you can only contribute a small amount to your savings each month when you are under 30, do it anyway: small amounts of money, if stored in high-interest accounts for long periods, can see their value doubled.

For example, let's imagine that you managed to save $10,000 before the age of thirty, and that you decided to deposit that amount in a high-interest account (4% per year). In five years, you would earn around $2,166.53. However, if you had saved that amount a year earlier, you would have earned about $500 more at the end of the same period, without any extra effort; a nice bonus if you ask us.

Don't get discouraged

When you can't save, it's easy to lose your mind. You may think you have no hope; you will believe that it is impossible to find the money you need to achieve your long-term goals. Remember, however, that no matter how small your starting capital is, you can always start saving. The sooner you start, the sooner you will achieve financial stability.

If you are worried about your financial situation, ask for help from an advisory service. These agencies, which often operate for free or for very low fees, can help you start saving.

Eliminate luxury goods from your budget

If you're having trouble saving money, this is the best place to start. Many of the expenses we take for granted are not essential at all. Eliminating the expense of luxury goods is a great first step to improving your financial situation, because it does not significantly alter the quality of your life or the ability to do your job. While it can be hard to imagine your days without a sports car and a Netflix subscription, you may be surprised at how easy it is to get on without those things when they are no longer a part of your life.

Find a cheaper home

For almost all people, housing costs represent the largest expense item in the budget. Therefore, saving in this area can allow you to dispose of a large part of your salary for other important items, such as retirement. While it is not always easy to move house, you should do a careful analysis of your expenses if you are unable to meet the budget you have imposed on yourself.

If you rent, try renegotiating with your landlord to snag a lower price. Many landlords want to avoid the risk of having to look for other tenants, so you may be able to get a better deal if you have a good relationship with your landlord.

If you need to pay a mortgage, talk to the bank about getting a refinance. You may be able to snatch a more favorable deal if your credit is stable. When you decide to refinance a loan, try not to extend the duration of the installments too much.

You may want to consider moving to areas where housing is cheaper.

Eat cheap

Many people spend more than they need to on food. While it's easy to forget budget constraints when biting into steak at your favorite restaurant, food-related expenses can go up a lot if you don't keep them in check. In general, buying in bulk is more profitable in the long run than buying small quantities of food; if you spend a lot on meals, you can decide to buy from wholesalers who supply restaurants. The most expensive option of all is to eat in restaurants, so try to eat at home as often as possible to save money.

Choose inexpensive and nutritious foods. Instead of buying ready-made and processed foods, try checking your supermarket's fresh food department. You might be surprised how cheap it is to eat healthy! For example, you can buy brown rice, a nutritious and very filling food, for less than one dollar per kilo.

Take advantage of discounts. Many supermarkets (especially large chains) distribute coupons and discounts at the checkout. Don't waste them!

If you often eat at a restaurant, stop doing it. Preparing a meal at home almost always costs a lot less than ordering it at a restaurant. Furthermore, by cooking your own dishes, you will also learn a useful skill that will allow you to entertain friends, satisfy relatives and even attract potential romantic companions.

If your situation is really bad, don't be ashamed to take advantage of the free food option. The soup kitchens offer meals to people in need. If you need help, consult your local authorities for more information.

Consume less energy

Most people accept the price of the bill without worrying about it. In reality, however, it is possible to greatly reduce energy consumption with a few simple steps. These tips are so mundane that there's no reason not to follow them if you want to save money. As an added benefit, consuming less energy reduces the amount of pollution you indirectly produce, minimizing your impact on the environment.

Turn off the lights you don't need. There is no reason to keep the light on in a room where no one is around. Try leaving a note on the door if you have trouble remembering it.

Avoid using heating and air conditioning if they are not needed. If you are hot, open the windows or use a small fan. If you're cold, wear layered clothing, use a blanket, or turn on an electric heater.

Invest in good insulation. If you can afford substantial home improvements, replacing old insulation with highly efficient modern products can save you money in the long run by preventing hot or cool air inside the house from escaping.

If you can, invest in solar panels. This solution is an excellent investment for your future and that of the planet. Even though the installation cost is quite high, photovoltaic technology becomes cheaper with each passing year.

Use less expensive means of transportation. Owning, maintaining and fueling a car can take up a large part of your income. Depending on the amount of miles you drive, the price of fuel can be as high as several hundred euros per month. In addition, the car requires fees for taxes and maintenance. Instead of driving, use cheap (or free) alternatives. This allows you not only to save money, but also to exercise more and reduce the stress of the journey to work.

Consider public transport in your area. Depending on where you live, you may have cheap transportation available. In almost all cities there are subways, buses or trams that connect the various areas and to move from city to city you can take advantage of the bus or train. Consider walking or cycling to your work. If you live close enough to your workplace, these are excellent choices for free commuting, fresh air and exercise.

If you can't help but take the car, consider sharing your travel and expenses with colleagues. By doing so, each of the passengers will contribute to the cost of fuel and maintenance of the vehicle. Plus, you'll have someone to talk to on the way.

Have fun without breaking the bank

While you can cut the luxuries out of your life to cut down on personal expenses, you don't necessarily have to stop having fun if you're trying to save. Finding cheaper entertainment allows you to strike the perfect balance between fun and responsibility. You will be surprised how much fun you can have with just a few dollars, if you are creative enough!

Stay up to date on events in your community. Today, almost all cities publish calendars of events scheduled in the area on the internet. Often these events will be inexpensive or even free. For example, in a medium-sized city it is often possible to visit free art exhibits, attend outdoor screenings, and attend donation-based community events.

Avoid expensive addictions

Some bad habits can ruin your savings efforts. In worst-case scenarios, these habits can become severe addictions, almost impossible to defeat without help, and can even cause harm to your health. Protect your wallet (and your body) from these addictions by avoiding them right away.

Today, the dangerous effects of smoking are well known. For instance, smoking causes lung cancer, heart disease, heart attacks and other serious conditions. If that's not enough, cigarettes cost a lot - up to more than $5 per pack.

Furthermore, do not drink too much. While a drink with friends may not hurt you, drinking a lot on a regular basis can cause serious problems in the long run, such as liver damage, brain damage, weight gain, delirium, and even death. If that weren't enough, sustaining an addiction to alcohol is a major burden on your finances.

Start from the essentials

There are some things you can't do without: food, water, home, and clothing must be your top priorities. Of course, if you become homeless or hungry, it would be impossible to meet the rest of your financial goals. Therefore, always make sure you have enough cash for these minimum requirements before you dedicate your money to anything else.

Just because food, water, and shelter are important doesn't mean you should spend everything you earn on those needs. For example, reducing the number of dinners at restaurants is a way to greatly reduce food spending. For the same reasons, moving to an area where rents or house prices are lower is a great way to save on your home.

Depending on the area you live in, housing expenses can make up a large chunk of your income. In general, most experts advise against moving into a home that requires more than a third of your income for expenses.

Pay your debts

If you don't keep them in check, they can completely ruin your savings efforts. If you paid off your debts at the minimum rate, you would end up spending a lot more money than if you paid back the sum that was loaned to you in less time. Save money in the long run by dedicating a good chunk of your income to paying off debts so you can pay them off as quickly as possible. As a general rule, paying high-interest mortgages first is the most effective way to use your money.

When you've covered essential expenses and created an emergency fund, you can safely devote almost all of the rest of your income to paying off your debts. If you don't have an emergency fund, you might decide to split the extra income between debt and the fund.

If you are indebted to multiple institutions and are unable to pay all the installments, you can consider consolidating your debt. You could sort all of your debts into one loan with a lower interest rate. It is important to note, however, that the payments for consolidated debts are almost always higher than the initial ones.

You can try to negotiate directly with the institution that granted you the loan to reduce the interest rate. The creditor does not benefit from bankrupting you, because they would lose their entire investment. Therefore, they could give you a lower interest rate to allow you to pay off your debt.

Spend in a smart way

After you've set aside a good percentage of your income as savings, if you still have money to spend, you can make non-essential investments to increase your productivity, earning potential, and quality of life over the long term. While these types of purchases aren't as essential as water, food, and household bills, they're smart choices that can save you money over time.

For example, buying an ergonomic chair for your office is not essential, but it is a smart choice in the long run, because it allows you to work harder and minimize back pain. Another example is replacing your old water heater. Even if the model you have works in the short term, by purchasing a new one you will not have to incur expenses for the maintenance of the previous one.

Leave luxury goods for last

Saving does not mean living an austere and joyless life. When you've paid off your debts, created an emergency fund, and spent your money on smart purchases that will benefit you in the long run, it's okay to dedicate some money to yourself. Healthy and responsible luxuries keep you from going crazy when you put your heart and soul into work, so don't be afraid to celebrate your financial stability with a few frivolous purchases.

Luxuries include anything that is not an essential commodity and offers no long-term benefit. This broad category includes travel, restaurant dinners, a new car, a satellite TV subscription, expensive gadgets, and more.

If you follow these steps, in a short period of time you will build a solid emergency fund. Once you have put aside at least 6 months worth of expenses, you can start working on your investments.

Chapter 2

Inflation or Why You Have to Invest

When it comes to investing, the first question everyone should ask themselves is "why should I even bother to invest?". After all, just saving up a part of your income seems a nice strategy for a bright future. However, this is not enough, because it does not take into consideration the greatest enemy of your finances: inflation.

With inflation in the economy, we mean the prolonged increase in the general average level of prices of goods and services over a given period of time, which generates a decrease in the purchasing power of money.

As prices rise, each monetary unit will be able to buy fewer goods and services. Consequently, inflation is also an erosion of consumers' purchasing power.

Inflation can have several causes, and there is no complete agreement on which one affects the most. Obviously, when the increase in the money supply is greater than the increase in the production of goods and services, we see inflation skyrocketing. Now, just consider that over 1 trillion dollars have been printed in 2020 and you can understand why there will be a problem in the near future.

According to John Maynard Keynes, inflation depends on demand, which, however, can grow regardless of the quantity of money injected if we are in a situation of full employment. In this case, in fact, demand grows due to the growth of wages.

The economist Luigi Einaudi also agreed on the negative view of inflation. On several occasions he has defined inflation as the most unfair of taxes because it affects the weaker classes to a greater extent. The increase in the general level of prices causes a loss of the purchasing power of money, because with the same quantity of money it is possible to buy a smaller quantity of goods and services.

The increase in the general price level expressed in percentage terms is the rate of inflation. Inflation has positive and negative effects. The current mainstream economy considers a moderate amount of positive inflation. For example, the European Central Bank has set a target of 2% inflation. Olivier Blanchard, chief economist of the International Monetary Fund believes that this limit could be raised to 4% to give the central bank more leeway in the event of a crisis. There is no shortage of schools of economic thought that consider higher inflation also appropriate, at least in some situations. Hyperinflation, on the other hand, is unanimously considered in a negative way.

Inflation entails the loss of value of the accumulated money, and unexpected inflation entails a transfer of wealth that is advantageous for those in a debt position and disadvantageous for those in a credit position. For example, a company or a single citizen who has contracted a debt with a fixed nominal interest rate benefits from an unexpected increase in inflation, if it also corresponds to a nominal increase in its income. The opposite happens for the bank that granted the loan, which gets back money with a lower value than budgeted. If, on the other hand, inflation is stable, the lender takes it into account when granting the loan, including the recovery of inflation in the nominal interest rate, in order to have a real positive interest rate.

Inflation in antiquity

There are many inflationary periods in ancient history. The first of these historically attested periods dates back to the Ancient Kingdom of Egypt and the Late Sumerian Period, around 2100 BC.

Another historically documented period of inflation coincided with the discovery of silver mines in Spain along the Rio Tinto and the Guadalquivir river by the Phoenicians, between 730 BC and 620 BC. At the time, Phenicia was subjected to the Assyrians and the massive importation of large quantities of silver into the Middle East caused the vertical collapse of the value of the metal, so much so that Assyria itself had to intervene to prevent further imports of Hispanic silver by garrisoning the ports of Ugarit, Sidon, Tire and Byblos.

Another historical episode of inflation occurred in Phrygia under King Midas whose mythical touch that transformed everything into gold echoes both the opulence of that people and the damage caused by an excess of wealth.

The annual inflation of 400 - 500% devastated the daily life of the inhabitants of Babylon and the Second Babylonian Empire between 580 B and 538 BC (date of the conquest of the city by the king of Persia, Cyrus the Great). Such high inflation reduced the earnings of farmers and merchants, so as to push the last Chaldean sovereigns to try to take possession of Arabia. The intent was to "mitigate" the price regime with the proceeds of spices in transit along the homonymous "spice route" in the hands of the Babylonians in the last stretch, between the Oasis of Tabuk and the city of Hegra. The failure to resolve the age-old problem of inflation was one of the causes of the lack of popular participation in the defense of the city against the Persians, as evidenced by some contemporary clay tablets.

Also during the Peloponnesian War between Athens and Sparta there was a period of severe inflation associated with recession due to the persistence of the war that deprived artisans and farmers from work and trade. With the definitive Spartan victory, at the end of the thirty-year conflict, the Laconic city was literally submerged by "owls" (from the coinage represented on the Athenian silver drachma of the period), which caused the subversion of the Spartan economy which, notoriously, forbade the use of money and the practice of trade.

During the period of decline of the Persian Empire, between 450 BC. and 330 BC, the continuous internal wars and the autonomist revolts forced the issue of notable quantities of local currency in order to pay the mercenary armies hired for this purpose.

In the period of conquest of the Persian Empire by Alexander the Great, the huge quantities of precious metals stolen from the subjugated and diverted countries in Greece, Macedonia and Epirus caused a decrease in the intrinsic value of the gold contained in the Persian Daricus and the silver of the Greek Drachma.

Subsequently, during the period passed into history with the name of "Hellenism", there was a generalized inflation of the "free currency" of the time, the Greek tetradrachm, following an uncontrolled issue of the same by the various kingdoms in which the empire of Alexander the Great was shattered.

A very serious inflation occurred during the late republican period in ancient Rome when the state, in order to continue to finance military campaigns, altered the metal alloy of the coins by lowering the quantity of precious metal contained in them.

An even worse situation occurred between the 2nd century AD and the definitive fall of the Western Roman Empire, in 476. During the course of the lower empire, there were such marked alterations in the securities of precious metal that many traders refused to be paid in money for the goods offered for sale and also many military personnel preferred payment in kind for services rendered. For example, at the time of the reign of Constantine I (312 - 337), the bronze axis was reduced to a size equal to 1/4 of the republican one of three hundred years earlier. Similar alterations underwent the silver denarius and the silver and gold sestertius. Constantine, in order to pay the soldiers, was forced to have the solid aureo minted: a coin containing a massive gold quantity. In this case, the monetary hinge of ancient Rome was represented by the Denarius, a coin that in 218 BC contained 4.5 grams of pure silver and was traded against ten bronze axes. Around 120 BC it was traded against sixteen bronze boards. The silver content of the denarius, around 210 AD was further reduced, coming to represent only 0.5% of the weight of the coin. This was offset by a surge in inflation that reached 1,000% over the years.

From Constantine onwards the denarius practically lost all value. Previously, thirty years earlier, the

Dalmatian emperor Diocletian introduced a basket of controlled goods. These were basic necessities that could not, by law, increase in price beyond a threshold set by the authorities policy, with the result that these goods were no longer available on the market, unless they were paid at much higher prices than those politically imposed. In the last decades of the empire, no one was willing to carry out the task of tax collector, a profession that was once very profitable, so much so that state officials had to be forced to do it. The emperors who devalued the silver coin were Nero, Caracalla, and Marcus Aurelius. Constantine abolished the silver Denarius because it was now devoid of effective value and substituted the Solid for the Aureus. But the Aureus contained 8.0 grams of fine gold, while the solid contained just over half of this quantity. The adulteration of the Solid traced that of the Denarius, so much so that the last Roman emperors of the West no longer even minted the solid, but the Tremisse, with a value of 1/3 of a solid, as it contained no more than 1.72 grams of gold .

Inflation in the Middle Ages

During the early Middle Ages the European economy was a survival economy, where autarchy and barter prevailed. With the monetary reform of Charlemagne, implemented around 770 - 780 AD, the lira was introduced both as a unit of measurement and as a unit of account. With this "virtual currency" , in an era of severe destitution and widespread poverty, about 47 plots of land could be bought for a single coin.

In the Late Middle Ages the Italian municipalities began to mint gold coins, and other European states also set out on this path. However, the counterfeiting of coins also began with a consequent resumption of inflation. For those who altered the currency - in any way and in any form - the death penalty was provided. A period of high inflation also occurred after 1352, when - at the end of the period in which the "Black Plague" raged in Europe, the population was halved compared to 1347 and - with the loss of about 30 million people - the peasants were able to obtain significant wage increases. Even the "War of the Roses", a civil war limited only to the aristocratic classes, from 1455 to 1485, left an inflationary aftermath in England after the Hundred Years War.

Inflation in modern history

The first major inflationary episode in modern history occurred at the end of the sixteenth century and led to a generalized rise in prices in Europe. There is a historiographical debate on the causes that determined it. According to some sources the reason was the Spanish exploitation of gold in the New World. In fact, following the plundering of the conquistadors at the expense of the Maya and Inca populations and the mining from deposits of the New World, the Spanish royal coffers found themselves in possession of huge quantities of gold, silver and precious goods that were poured into the European markets both to arm the army and to hire mercenaries.

The most colossal European monetary scam, which resulted in the total loss of value of the French currency, involved numerous mints that supplied the Ottoman Empire. Beginning in 1656, Ottoman women began to adorn themselves with earrings, bracelets and necklaces made with the French silvery Luigino. The coin was initially minted by the Paris mint for King Louis XIV from 1643. The undoubted beauty of the French coinage struck Muslim women, so much so that the demand for the French currency grew exponentially, as in Constantinople the wealthiest families were willing to pay a price even double the intrinsic value of the coin, given its silver content.

Faced with the possibility of large earnings, the French mints authorized to mint the coin were multiplied, but also mints located outside the French borders, by virtue of previous acquired rights, began to mint export coins. Meanwhile, in Turkey, the amount of luigini poured out meant that other jewels, starting with the rings of the various governors, were made with the luigini. The flood of luigini, however, depleted the French state coffers with silver, so much so that the king himself had to intervene to block its issue and marketing in 1667.

In the meantime, the sale of "unofficial" luigini continued, containing metal more and more debased by silver, so much so that a diplomatic crisis between

Turkey and France took place. In fact, the Turkish sultan issued a decree that prohibited the importation of luigini. The circulation of an excessive quantity of coins in Turkey caused a surge in the price of basic necessities and the sultan had to intervene again, in 1667 to deflate the speculative bubble through the requisition and subsequent merger of the imported coins.

After the American War of Independence, the printing of quantities of paper money beyond any control produced an inflationary spiral such that even today, in the United States, the expression "No Continental" indicates an object of negligible value. In 1791 the exchange rate between Dollar and Gold was fixed at 19.49 Dollars per ounce and for over a century it remained at those levels. The first serious devaluation of the American currency occurred with President Roosevelt, who fixed the new exchange rate in 1933 at 35.00 Dollars per Ounce, in the aftermath of the severe Wall Street stock market crisis of 1929. The end of the "Gold Standard" occurred on the morning of August 15, 1971, when the American President Richard Nixon unilaterally abolished the fixed exchange rate between the Dollar and the gold ounce with immediate effect. Fifty years later, on April 25, 2021, the cost of an ounce of gold was around $1,483.62.

A further famous inflationary episode occurred shortly after the First World War in Germany, during the Weimar Republic, between 1919 and 1924. The payments in compliance with the ultimatum of London, which required the liquidation of enormous compensation for the damages of war in gold marks triggered a perverse spiral that led to a devaluation of the currency and to inflation at stratospheric rates. Wages and salaries were paid every day so that their value was not reduced to zero. Between June and December 1922, the cost of living rose 16 times.

The inflationary spiral meant that people, as soon as they were paid, ran to buy any kind of goods before finding themselves with money without real value in hand, thus aggravating the scarcity of goods in circulation. Hyperinflation was defeated with the issue of a new currency, the Rentenmark, guaranteed by the lands and goods of the industrialists, then replaced by the Reichsmark with equal exchange rates. Weimar hyperinflation is often directly connected with the rise of Hitler's Third Reich, even though hyperinflation was defeated as early as 1924, so almost ten years before the advent of Nazism.

On June 15, 1939, the German government approved the Reichsbankgesetz, the reform law that limited the decision-making autonomy of the Central Bank and obliged it to carry out the monetary policy indications, which returned to the powers of the executive.

After World War II, the Reichsbank was replaced by the Bundesbank and totally freed from political power. The German mark became the European reference currency, so much so that the Austrian schilling, the Danish krone and the Dutch guilder were linked to it by a fixed exchange rate.

In the twenty years between 1927 and 1946 there was a hyperinflationary episode in Hungary as well. At that time there was a currency in circulation, the pengő, which began to depreciate rapidly to cope with the huge war expenditures starting in 1938. After the Second World War, the pengő suffered the highest rate of hyperinflation ever recorded in history. It was re-evaluated, but this did not stop the hyperinflation and prices continued to rise out of control, forcing the issuance of ever higher banknote denominations. The largest denomination put into circulation was worth 1x1020 (= 100,000,000,000,000,000,000,000) pengő. The Hungarian economy could only be stabilized with the introduction of a new currency and on August 1st 1946 the Hungarian forint was introduced.

Inflation in contemporary age

Chronically affected by hyperinflation were the Latin American countries in the forty years between 1950 and 1990. In particular, an emblematic case is the situation of Brazil, where inflation has practically always accompanied national history. In 1930 the democratically elected president, Getúlio Vargas, assumed dictatorial powers in 1937 establishing a concept of corporatist state which lasted until the deposition of Vargas himself in 1945. In 1942 the new cruzeiro was introduced in Brazil, divided into 100 centavos remained in circulation until 1967, which replaced the "real" at a rate of 1 mil réis = 1 cruzeiro. After a further four years with Vargas at the helm of the country, a military coup d'état in 1964 brought a military junta to the government. Meanwhile, inflation got out of control.

As a result of rising inflation, in 1967 the old cruzeiro was replaced by the new cruzeiro, at a rate of 1 new cruzeiro = 1000 old cruzeiro. After the fall of the dictatorial junta following massive street demonstrations in Rio de Janeiro and Sao Paulo, in 1984, the democratic government, in 1986, abolished the old currency and the new cruzeiro was replaced by the cruzado, at the rate of 1 000 new cruzeiro = 1 cruzado. Again, in 1989, the newborn cruzado was replaced by the new cruzado, at a rate of 1000 cruzado = 1 new cruzado. And again, in 1990, Brazil returned to using the name cruzeiro for its currency: the third cruzeiro replaced the second cruzado at par. And therefore, on August 1st 1993 the third cruzeiro was replaced by the "cruzeiro real" with a rate of devaluation so fast that it forced the Brazilian currency to be pegged to the US dollar. In 1994 the cruzeiro real was replaced by the second real at the rate of 1 real = 2 750 cruzeiro real.

As for Bolivia in 1985 annual inflation settled at 11,750%. The end of the civil war in Nicaragua left the country an annual inflation of 13,109%, while three years later, Peru experienced an inflation rate of 7,482%.

Mexico between 1994 and 1995 suffered a series of financial speculative attacks against its currency, the Peso, which depreciated - in one year - by 35% against the US dollar. Only the allocation of US monetary aid, resulting from the collapse of the profits of the US multinationals themselves, blocked financial speculation and revived the Mexican currency.

After 1991, with the end of communism, a situation of rapid loss of value of the currency took place in Russia and in the countries of Eastern Europe. In fact, in a market essentially closed and without competition, statalized and politically controlled such as that of the Soviet Union and the satellite countries, the opening to the free market regime caused a return to the regime of barter and the refusal of payment with national currencies. Russia only recovered from the financial abyss with the appointment of Vladimir Putin as prime minister in 1998. Also worthy of mention are the cases of Serbia between 1987 and 1994 and of Zimbabwe starting from 1984.

Causes of inflation

In the study of macroeconomics, the causes of inflation are generally identified in these three categories.

- Demand inflation. It happens when an excess of demand for goods and services relative to the supply of goods and services causes prices to rise, if and until production fails to adjust. It is the Keynesian explanation.
- Cost inflation. This refers to the increase in production costs, especially of raw materials and labor, which provokes the reaction of companies that increase the selling prices of products.

- Excess money inflation. Monetarist theory attributes inflation to the uncontrolled expansion of the money supply by central banks.

As you can see from the examples we just made, inflation happens when there is uncertainty and doubt in the future. If you have not lived under a rock the past few months, you know what is happening in the world and how the global economy has been damaged. Trillions of dollars were printed in 2020 and will be printed in the coming years. There is no doubt inflation will rise again in the near future and the only thing you can do to protect yourself against it is to invest. In fact, assets increase in value when the purchasing power of currencies decreases.

Now that you understand why you cannot just save up your way to a comfortable future life, we can dive deeper into how to invest in the stock market.

Chapter 3

What is a Stock?

A stock is a financial security representing a share of the ownership of a public limited company. Together with bonds and derivatives, it is part of the transferable securities investment category. The owner is called a shareholder and the set of shares in the company is called "share capital".

It is a form of financial investment, which exposes the invested capital to a certain amount of risk.

Companies need money to carry out their business activities and accumulate profits over time to carry out further activities, make investments and grow. There are two ways to raise funds: debt financing and non-debt financing. Through debt, bank loans are used and need to be repaid with accrued interest. As an alternative, corporate bonds can be issued.

The alternative to debt financing is equity financing. The collection of non-debt loans takes place through the sale of shares. In ancient times, the share was a certified piece of paper certifying the payment of its value and the possession of a part of the entire share capital of the company. The buyers, by buying these financial products that looked like pieces of paper, each paid a part of all the capital. For example, if you issue 10 shares worth $100 each and one shareholder buys 4 and the second shareholder buys 6, a total of $1000 is collected; the first shareholder pays $400, while the second pays $600. The former owns 40% of the share capital, while the latter, owning 60%, is the majority shareholder; on the other hand, the former is a minority shareholder.

The ultimate goal of buying shares is manifold. First of all, the purchase of these valuable pieces of paper allows companies to receive capital and encourages entrepreneurship; it allows the carrying out of activities as companies can cover their costs; if these activities are successful and bring revenues such that the cost of the activities is covered and a profit is generated, this profit serves the company to grow or carry out more and more activities or repay debts in the medium and long term. Finally, it serves the shareholders themselves to capitalize on the success of the company they have financed with equity.

To be precise, a few times a year, part of the profits generated by the company is redistributed through dividends to shareholders. According to the plutocratic principle, the profits allocated are divided according to the shareholding: the majority shareholder who paid 60% of the money as they bought 60% of the shares, are entitled to 60% of the profits. The minority shareholder who paid the remaining 40% is entitled to 40%.

In addition, the value of the share can fluctuate over time as it can rise or fall. The shareholder, including speculators and those who practice day trading, can also earn by reselling their shareholding to a new shareholder. For example, if the majority shareholder who bought 6 shares worth $100 each and spent $600 waits for the company to generate profits, they can see how the value of a single share doubles from $100 to $200. €. Thus, they can resell their stake for $1200 and earn $600, without needing to receive dividends.

The share is a non-debt financing as the money does not have to be repaid, but the gain for the shareholder derives from the distribution of dividends. The latter are obtainable if the business and investment activities are successful, which is not at all obvious as they can be a failure. A high dividend profit is a risky premium.

The difference between a share and a corporate bond can be found in the earning mechanism and in the risk. The bond is a loan of money by an investor, the bondholder. The company, by the bond maturity date, must repay the money with accrued interest. The bond's interest rate rises if the investment is risky (e.g. the company is already heavily indebted) or based on a low rating from the appropriate agencies justified by high debts or habitual breach of covenants. If the interests are very high and the risk is very high, we are talking about junk-bonds.

Shares, bonds and derivatives (futures, options, SWAPs) are all three parts of a class of financial products called securities; stocks are equity securities, while bonds are debt securities.

Since the shares can be freely resold to new shareholders, they are said to be negotiable securities. In addition, since they can be sold quickly they are easily liquidable investments.

Shares and other securities are traded in unofficial, private and less regulated markets and channels, i.e. over the counter OTC and, alternatively, in the public, official and regulated market created specifically to exchange securities. There are various exchanges around the world, and in order to trade shares of a particular company on the stock exchange, the company must first be registered on it. The listing takes place only if the company complies with certain requirements, e.g. have a share capital not below a certain threshold. A company can also unsubscribe from one exchange (delisting) or transfer from one exchange to another (translisting) or go public on two exchanges (double listing). When a company goes public and issues its first shares in the public market, these shares are launched through what is called an Initial Public Offering IPO.

Today these securities are dematerialized. They are no longer pieces of paper, but virtual data and the sale takes place through online trading platforms and no longer in person on the stock exchange or by telephone.

All the money raised with the shares issued is called "market capitalization", or simply market cap.

The set of all stock trading forms, in an abstract sense, the stock market, which is therefore part of the securities market (stock market, bond market and derivatives market).

The purchasers of shares can be common savers, large professional investors, other companies (eg banks, corporations, insurance companies, etc.), the State and the management of the company itself. The latter can therefore enjoy the fruits of their diligent and non-opportunistic work through dividends (think for example of a manager who wastes company money to buy a luxury car for himself). In general, workers can be directly involved in the shareholding with specific plans called Employee Stock Ownership Plan (ESOP), with which they are paid in shares from which dividends derive or the possibility of reselling them when they increase in value.

If the collection of equity loans takes place over the counter, we speak of private equity financing. Otherwise if it occurs on the stock exchange we speak of public equity financing.

In conclusion, there are several types of shares. Ordinary shares are the basic ones and, by buying them, the shareholder also has the power to vote in the shareholders' meeting when important decisions are made on the future of the company. The value of the vote is calibrated on the basis of the number of shares purchased or, in most cases, this standard is not explicitly followed in favor of the plutocratic principle: if the majority shareholder has paid 60% of the share capital, regardless of the number of shares bought, their vote alone is worth 60 out of 100.

Preferred shares give the right of precedence over ordinary shareholders when distributing dividends but, as a counterpoint, they take away the right to vote.

Although there is a hierarchy in the order of the distribution of dividends, all shareholders have the right to participate in the profits regardless of the order as there is the absolute prohibition of the Leonine Agreement.

If the company goes bankrupt and once the credit renegotiations and the initiatives to save it from inside or outside (employee buyout, management buyout, etc.) have failed, the shareholders are entitled to receive the money remaining from the liquidation of the company. The first to get paid are those who are entitled to compensation following a trial. Then come the banks. If anything remains, it then goes to the suppliers and bondholders. Finally, assuming that something remains, the shareholder's turn comes.

As you can see, investing in stocks is quite risky and it exposes your capital to potential losses. However, if you decide not to invest, your capital is going to depreciate over time due to inflation. Therefore, you have no choice but to invest. The only thing you can do is to try to mitigate risk, by studying the other chapters of this book and applying effective investing strategies.

Chapter 4

Index Funds

As we have seen in the previous chapter, investing in single stocks can be quite risky. However, not investing at all leads to a certain loss in purchasing power due to inflation. Therefore, the investor needs to find a way to invest without putting the capital at too much risk. Index funds try to solve the problem.

A stock index is a summary of the value of the basket of stocks it represents. The movements of the index are a good approximation of the variation over time in the valuation of the securities included in the portfolio. There are different methods of calculating the index, depending on the weighting that is attributed to the shares in the basket.

Different types of index funds

A distinction is made between these types of index funds.

- **Value weighted indexes**. Each stock is proportional to its market capitalization. Unlike other calculation methods, in this case the indexes are adjusted following corporate transactions such as splits, groupings, payment of extraordinary dividends, and so on.

- **Equally weighted indices.** These are characterized by the equality of the weighting factors for all the stocks that make up the index. The capitalization of the companies included does not matter, because all the stocks in the index have the same weight.

- **Price weighted indexes.** In this case the weight associated with each security varies according to its price. If the price of a security increases more than the others, its weight within the index also automatically increases. They are very simple to calculate as they are given by the simple sum of the prices of the securities that make up the index. However, these indexes have the disadvantage of not correctly reflecting the performance of the entire portfolio. In fact, the most "expensive" securities are represented more, regardless of the number of shares and the size of the company.

- **Sustainability indexe.** These indexe weigh each security according to alternative principles to economic and dimensional criteria and introduce CSR (Corporate Social Responsibility) evaluations or more purely socio-environmental analysis. Very often they are elaborated by the same companies that elaborate the major indexes, such as the Dow Jones Sustainability World Index or the STOXX ESG.

Most of the major world indexes are calculated using the value weighted methodology. These include the American S&P 500 and the Nyse Composite indexes. Equity indexes can also be classified according to the industrial sector to which the securities in the portfolio refer or the geographical area to which they belong.

Almost all the indexes are calculated on the basis of the market price. This system, however, partially distorts reality, as the remuneration that companies give to their shareholders is not considered in full, but only that granted as capital gain. Dividends, in fact, are not taken into account and on the ex-dividend day the shares undergo a nominal depreciation which in theory should be equal to the dividend paid. Therefore, when an index based only on stock market prices records a decline, the greater the it is the more generous the dividend is. In this way, an event that is welcomed by investors appears to be negative. To give an example, on May 22nd, 2006 as many as 24 S&P companies cut dividends and the effect weighed 1.547% on the list, nominally amplifying the drops of that day. To remedy this deficiency, the so-called total return indexes are spreading. These also take into account the reinvestment of dividends and other cash flows deriving from the possession of these securities.

In the next few chapters we are going to dive deeper into some of the most famous index funds and talk about their history.

Chapter 5

The Dow Jones Industrial Average

The Dow Jones Industrial Average also known as the DJIA or Dow 30, is a stock index that hosts 30 major companies listed on the New York Stock Exchange. The DJIA is the second largest market index in the United States in terms of age and is characterized as an index designed to serve as an indicator of the economic health of the United States and the world economy in general terms.

Within the Dow Jones we find large companies such as General Motors, Goodyear, IBM and Amgen. If these companies in the index have a positive return, it means that the country's economy is "doing well". If, on the other hand, the economy "is bad", prices tend to fall.

Therefore, the Dow Jones acts as a sample of market trends as a whole. This becomes relevant if we consider the US economy is able to generate trends at a global level.

The composition of the Dow Jones

The index evaluation is often performed to replace companies that no longer meet the correct listing criteria. The composition of the index has changed about 60 times since the launch of the first 30 components, especially in its early years in the aftermath of the Great Depression.

For example, in 1932 eight of the components were replaced within the Dow Jones, and it was the first large-scale change. Due to the changes generated by the 2020 pandemic, three changes were made on August 24, in which companies Salesforce, Amgen and

Honeywell replaced Exxon Mobil, Pfizer and Raytheon Technologies.

How it is calculated

When the index was launched in 1896, it was made up of only 12 companies, mainly focused on the industrial sector such as railways, cotton, gas, sugar, tobacco and oil.

With the evolution of the economy, the composition of the index has changed. The Dow makes changes when a company loses relevance to current economic trends or when there is a very large economic change and the change will thus be reflected within the index. For example, if a company loses a percentage of its market capitalization due to certain financial difficulties, it is liable to be removed from the index.

The weighting that is carried out in the index is based on the share price. In other words, a stock will be more relevant in the index the more value it will have on the market.

This is known as Dow Divisor, a predetermined constant used to determine the effect of a one-point move in any of the 30 stocks that make up the index. The current divisor found in the Wall Street Journal is 0.14748071991788.

The Dow is not calculated with an arithmetic mean and does not take into account market capitalization, as other indexes do. Instead, it reflects the sum of a share price for all its components divided by the Dow Divisor.

DJIA Price = SUM (Component Share Prices) / Dow Divider

For example, if the stock of one company goes up from $100 to $110 and the stock of a second company goes down from $11 to $10, the Dow will increase overall, even if the first member is up 10% and the second member fell by 10%.

Historic milestones

Here are some important historical milestones reached by the Dow.

- **1933.** March 15th saw the highest percentage gain in one day, as the Dow gained 8.26 points to close at +62.10% for the day.

- **1987.** On October 19th, also known as Black Monday, there was the highest percentage drop in one day, as the index fell by 22.61%.

- **2001**. September 17th is the fourth largest drop in points in a day, due to the events of September 11th. The Dow fell 684.81 points that day, which represents a drop close to 7.1%.

- **2013**. On May 3rd, the Dow crossed the 15,000 mark for the first time in history.

- **2017.** On January 25th, the Dow Jones closed above 20,000 points for the first time in history.

- **2018.** January 4th 2018 the Dow Jones closed above 25,000 points for the first time in history.

- **2019**. On July 11th the Dow surpassed 27,000 for the first time in its history.

- **2020**. On February 12th, 2020, the Dow reached a new all-time high of 29,551 points.

- **March 2020.** Due to the pandemic, the Dow dropped below 20,000 points and lost more than 3,000 points in a single day.

The limits of the Dow Jones index

There is a certain group of economic analysts who are critical of the Dow Jones Index, as they argue for a lack of meaningful representation in determining the health of the US economy. They argue that 30 large-cap companies cannot be the basis for analyzing the country's economy, as they neglect companies of different sizes.

For this reason, many prefer to have as a reference the S&P 500, which includes 500 companies, which gives them greater scope for diversification.

To make matters worse, some critics also believe that just taking the share price may not reflect a company in the way the market capitalization factor does. In other words, the price of a stock could be overvalued, greatly affecting the accuracy of the Dow Jones index.

Chapter 6

The Standard & Poor's 500

The Standard & Poor's 500 is the most important North American stock index. Although historically the Dow Jones index originated first, this basket has taken on greater importance for investors over time. It is the leading equity benchmark for listed stocks on Wall Street and is the underlying for an incredibly wide range of derivative products, such as futures, options and certificates.

This index, created by Standard & Poor's has been calculated since March 4, 1957 thanks to the advanced and complex calculation capabilities possible with advances in the field of electronics. Before 1957, when there were still no computers, in fact, the S&P index contained only 90 stocks.

Membership requirements

The S&P 500 contains 500 shares of the same number of companies listed in New York (NYSE and Nasdaq), representing approximately 80% of the market capitalization, which are selected by a special committee. In reality, there are 505 securities in the basket as two types of shares are listed for 5 companies. All the securities in question relate to US companies with a market capitalization of more than $6.1 billion, a free float of at least 50%, a monthly trading volume of not less than 250,000 shares and a value annual average of the stock greater than 1.0 dollar.

Although most of these titles relate to US companies, the geographic criterion is still not a discriminating factor.

The companies to be included in the basket are selected through the floating capitalization method.

Originally the weights of the components of the index depended on the mere capitalization of the companies, but starting from 2005 the principle of floating capitalization was introduced. The transition to the new calculation system, due to the large number of stocks in the index, was carried out in two stages, the first on March 18th, 2005 and the second on September 16th of the same year. However, this change did not lead to a major upheaval. In fact, the S&P 500 companies with a free float lower than the total capitalization are a small minority.

The main titles

All stocks included in the S&P 500 are also part of the other extended S&P 1500 baskets, which includes S&P MidCap 400 and S&P SmallCap 600, and the S&P Global 1200.

The 10 stocks that currently have a greater weight in the basket and that together reach approximately 21% of the total, are Apple, Microsoft Corp, Amazon, Berkshire Hathaway, Johnson & Johnson, JP Morgan Chase, Facebook, Exxon Mobil, Alphabet C and Alphabet A. As regards the individual sectors, the most represented are that of IT with 20.7%, health care with 15.0% and financials with 13.6%.

Due to the large number of stocks included in the index, the numerous funds that use it as a benchmark rarely exactly replicate the portfolio of 500 stocks, since the sales would require significant costs in terms of brokerage fees. Portfolio managers usually use the synthetic replication technique. This means that they try to replicate the performance of the index with a smaller number of stocks selected on the basis of complex algorithms. Alternatively, many money managers use the very liquid futures that have this index as an underlying and that are listed on the Chicago Mercantile Exchange.

Trading hours

The value of the S&P 500 is automatically calculated every 15 seconds on the basis of the prices of the last contracts concluded in the trading hours, i.e. from 09:30 to 16:00 from Reuters America, a Thomson Reuters Corporation company.

The index code on the American markets is GSPC or SPX. It is sometimes also referred to as ^GSPC or ^SPX.

Chapter 7

The Nasdaq Composite

The NASDAQ Composite is a capitalization weighted index. The calculation of the index involves the calculation of the weighted sum of the products of the closing prices of the securities. This sum is divided by a divisor which reduces the order of magnitude of the result. For a stock to be included in the Nasdaq Composite, it must be listed exclusively on the Nasdaq stock market, unless the stock was listed at least twice on a non-US market prior to 2004 and has been listed continuously.

The index was introduced in 1971, with an initial value of 100 points. On July 17th 1995 it closed for the first time with a value greater than 1000 points. During the period of the dot-com bubble, the value of the index increased by 400%. On March 10th 2000 it reached the value of 5132.52. In the following period, the value underwent a significant decline, reaching 1,108.49 in October 2002. Until 2007, the index saw a decrease in its value. On September 15th, 2008, the bankruptcy of Lehman Brothers led the index to register a negative performance -3.6%, the worst percentage drop in a single session.

In the years following the Great Recession, the index returned to high values. On March 2nd 2015, for the first time since March 9th 2000, it closed with a value above 5000 points. In April 2015, closing at 5056, it exceeded the value reached during the dot-com bubble. On January 2nd, 2018 it exceeded the value of 7000 points and in 2019 the index had an increase of 35.2%, closing the year at 8972.60 points. On March 23rd 2020, the index touched a low of 6860 points. In the following months, however, there was a strong recovery in the index and on June 9th 2020, the index exceeded 10,000 for the first time in its history.

As you have learned in these chapters, index funds are a great way to invest in the stock market while mitigating risk. But how can you get started investing in them? Well, that is when ETFs come into play.

Chapter 8

The Secret Weapon: ETFs

Exchange-traded funds (known by the abbreviation ETF) are a type of investment funds listed on the stock exchange, with limited liability for the shareholders who participate in them with the purchase and sale of shares. Furthermore, they have the fundamental peculiarity of being passively managed since they are linked to a pre-existing stock index.

They are part of the family of exchange-traded products (ETPs), which include ETFs (exchange-traded funds), ETCs (exchange-traded commodities) and ETNs (exchange-traded notes), all three listed on the stock exchange and funded through shares.

Exchange-traded funds are a type of investment fund. This means they are an accumulation of money raised through the shareholding of shareholders. The fund is managed by a manager, to whom the shareholders delegate all management power. The ETF manager invests the money raised in the trading of shares. In any case, the profit generated by the fund's investment activities is then redistributed to the shareholder to the extent that they have invested in the fund, following the plutocratic principle. For instance, if a shareholder has paid 12% of the share capital, at each distribution of dividends they are entitled to 12% of all profits generated. If the fund at a strategic level is already set up to reinvest profits, it is called an "accumulation ETF", otherwise it is called a "distribution ETF".

The funds operate on the stock exchange as they are listed there, which is why these funds identify well with "exchange-traded": the purchase and sale of the shareholding takes place on the stock exchange, which is a public and regulated market.

However, ETFs have a particular functioning, since management is not absolutely free but has its own underlying logic: ETFs replicate the index to which they refer and therefore faithfully replicate the performance of a specific stock index or the price of a specific type of asset. Since the investment strategy is passive, the fund is said to be passively managed and the same fund can be said to be "passive".

Their management is passive but, in some cases, it is speculative. This happens for example if they use leverage, or if they exploit a bearish trend by shorting the market. Speculative ETFs that use leverage are also known as "Leveraged ETFs" and are flanked by two other types of speculative ETFs. These are Inverse ETFs and Reverse Leveraged ETFs. Typically, the speculative ones seek the maximum profit in the shortest possible time, which is why they tend to be used in day trading, which from the outset, in addition to being purely speculative, is particularly risky.

An example of an ETF is the SPDR S&P 500 Trust ETF, which binds to the S&P 500 index. Therefore, the ETF manager in this case uses the members' money to invest in various ways in the 500 companies that belong to this stock index. From the name, it follows that, at the level of legal form according to corporate law, the companies that manage the funds can be structured as trusts. However, some funds can also link to indexes that have an international breadth. More than one ETF can be linked to the same stock or commodity or similar index. For example, many ETFs follow the S&P 500 index. In 2015, there were over 4,000 ETFs worldwide and their assets combined totaled $2.88 trillion; the largest is the SPDR S&P 500 Trust ETF, which is a multi-billionaire ETF. Another huge one is the iShares Core S&P 500 ETF managed by BlackRock, which itself manages many other ETFs and is structured like a public company. Each ETF is always listed on a stock exchange. For example, the iShares Core S&P 500 ETF is listed on the New York Stock Exchange.

Each ETF is then specialized as they track a particular stock market index, a specific sector, specific commodities, specific securities, market caps, regions and may combine various financial products. If you use a region-specific specialization and indicate it in the fund name, the word "ex-" indicates an exclusion:

for example, "Pacific ex-Japan" means all of the Pacific except Japan. The name can also indicate the financial product or commodity or sector on which one focuses. For instance Oil, Gas, Bond, Energy, and Health ETFs.

The price of the shares to participate in the ETF can fluctuate throughout the day and be volatile due to the continuous exchange of shares on the exchange from one buyer to another.

In general, ETFs have lower expenses and the commissions to be paid for brokers are lower. Therefore ETFs are cheaper than index funds, even if they replicate their performance. Furthermore, as there are many types of ETF, they allow a great diversification of the investment portfolio. The basic expense for participating in an ETF is the payment of an annual fee.

Other features of ETFs

ETFs are financial instruments that choose to invest in a diversified basket by faithfully "replicating" the composition of a stock market index: when one of the components of the benchmark is replaced, the corresponding financial asset within the fund is also replaced. It is important to note that the benchmark is followed regardless of the greater or lesser convenience. The ETF will be aligned to the components and weights of the benchmark without the need for investor intervention.

ETFs are traded on the stock exchange in continuous trading, like shares and consequently their value varies continuously within the same trading day. Continuously bringing the fund's share back to the level of that of the index is the job of the management company itself, which will buy or sell its shares of the ETF due to the deviation from the index, which it should generally not exceed 2%.

ETFs are very liquid instruments, easily tradable. For amounts up to $1,000,000, trading takes place easily on the stock market; for higher amounts it is necessary to operate OTC, i.e. outside the public and regulated market directly with a market maker.

Despite the passive management style, there have been times when ETFs have performed better on average than active funds.

The total annual fees range from a minimum of 0.09% to a maximum of 1.5% and are paid in proportion to the holding period of the ETF.

If you understand the power of diversification and the value of index investing, we are sure you cannot wait to get started with ETF investing. The next chapters are going to tell you the right strategies to maximize your gains.

Chapter 9

Advantages and Disadvantages of ETFs

Being comparable to mutual funds, the assets of the ETFs are autonomous and completely separate from that of the issuer. And this makes them safer than other forms of investment: in fact, the bankruptcy of an issuer does not involve any financial risk for the ETF's assets and, consequently, for the investor.

Now let's see in detail the advantages and disadvantages of ETFs.

Diversification

An ETF can give visibility to a group of stocks and market segments. Compared to a stock, the ETF is able to monitor a wider range of stocks, but also "mimic" the returns of a country or group of countries. For example, it is possible for the investor to focus on Brazil, Russia, India and China in the BRIC ETF. Mutual funds can also be diversified, but the ETF has lower expenses and "works" like an equity investment.

Lower fees than managed funds

ETFs have much lower expense ratios than other managed funds. The costs of a mutual fund are usually higher due to management fees, shareholder expenses for accounting, service fees, board of directors fees. administration and freight charges for sales and distribution. Even if the ETF could give the holder some diversification benefits, it is always traded as a share.

Dividends are reinvested immediately

Company dividends in an open-ended ETF are reinvested right away. This is a great advantage for those who want to build wealth without taking out dividends.

Tax efficiency

ETFs can be more tax efficient than mutual funds because most of the capital gains tax is paid on the sale and in full to the investor. Even if the ETF sells or buys shares while trying to mimic a basket of shares, it will always be monitored. This is so that the capital gains realized on the transfers do not give rise to a tax burden and can be expected to be much lower than normal mutual funds. Mutual funds, on the other hand, are required to distribute capital gains to shareholders if the manager sells securities to make a profit. This amount is calculated on the basis of the shareholder's percentage and is taxable as a capital gain. If other mutual fund holders sell them before the registration date, the remaining holders will split the capital gain and pay their taxes, even if the fund has dropped in value.

Low discount or premium on the price

There is a lower chance of having ETF prices that are higher or lower than the real value. These funds are traded throughout the day at a price close to that of the underlying securities, so if the price is significantly higher or lower than the net asset value, arbitrage will bring the price back "in line".

They can be limited to large companies

In some countries, investors may have limited access to these funds due to a small group of stocks in the large-cap market index. And this could limit the purchase of ETFs by small and medium-sized investors.

The daily price may be excessive

Longer-term investors may have a 10 or 15-year time horizon, so they cannot benefit from daily price changes. Some investors may trade more stocks due to these delayed price swings. And this "swing" could lead to a situation where prices at the end of the day could be irrational.

The supply-demand spread could be high

The more ETFs are created, the more you could "run into" an investment with a low volume index. A better price could be found in investing in real shares or perhaps even in a managed fund.

The costs, in fact, could be high. Most people make the mistake of comparing trading ETFs with trading other securities, such as mutual funds. However, when comparing ETFs that invest in a specific stock, the costs are higher. The actual commission paid to the broker may be the same, but there are no handling fees for the shares.

<u>Dividend yields</u>

Even though ETFs pay dividends to holders, the yields can never be as high as those of high yielding stocks or a group of stocks. The risks associated with managing ETFs are generally lower, but if an investor can take the risk, then the dividend yields can be much higher.

ETFs are a great way to invest in the stock market and the advantages outweigh the disadvantages. If you want to diversify your portfolio, but index funds are too expensive for you, then ETFs are the perfect solution for your needs.

Chapter 10

How to Choose an ETF

First of all, you have to choose the asset class. Do you want to invest in stocks, bonds, commodities or real estate mutual funds? If you are unsure what percentage of your portfolio should be allocated to each class, keep reading because we will give you an example portfolio in the next chapters.

The next step is to define your diversification strategy. Do you want to spread your wealth across all asset classes or do you want to focus on a single market segment? In equities, for example, you can invest worldwide with a single ETF or focus on certain regions, such as emerging markets or a single country.

After you have decided these points, here are the characteristics you need to keep an eye on when choosing an ETF.

Fund size over $100 million

A fund size of over $100 million should be preferred. The ETF is obliged to be profitable enough to be liquidated when it exceeds a certain threshold.

Fund age (over one year)

You can compare ETFs once they have accrued a reasonable set of historical data. You will need a performance history of at least one year, even better if you can focus on an observation period of three or five years.

Current expenses

The Total Expense Ratio (TER) offers us an approximate measure of the annual expenses that will have to be incurred in order to hold the ETF. It covers the various administrative, legal, operational and marketing expenses incurred by the ETF manager and deducted from the returns. The current expense index is another terminology used to indicate a similar concept.

The difference is that the TER considers all the costs that you will have to incur to own the ETF. The OCF, for example, does not include fees or taxes on operations.

These hidden costs have an impact on the ETF's annual return, so performance data can be used to make more accurate comparisons on the actual costs of ETFs.

Tracking differentials

The perfect ETF offers exactly the same return as the index that follows. Unfortunately, however, ETFs are subject to hurdles that have no impact on indexes. ETFs have to bear the costs of operations, taxes, wages and salaries, regulatory fees, and a long list of other costs. On the other hand, indexes are a kind of virtual world ranking therefore they can calculate returns in a market not affected by the deterrents of ETFs.

The difference between the real world returns of ETFs and the virtual returns of the index is called the tracking differential. A good ETF manages to minimize tracking spreads by offering a market return that is theoretically quite similar to that of the index minus its management costs.

The impact of tracking differentials can be assessed by comparing the ETFs that follow the same index over the same period of time. Just compare the overall returns with each other over a rather long period of time and you will see which ETF did a better job replicating the index.

Liquid assets

When we talk about liquidity we refer to the actual ease in being able to trade the ETF on a stock exchange. The more liquid the ETF is, the more likely it will be possible to sell or buy it with only a minimal cost. Broad market ETFs are usually very liquid as the underlying financial instruments they hold are regularly traded in very large volumes. For example, most equities traded on the NYSE stock market are highly liquid. Therefore, ETFs that hold these stocks can be traded very quickly by paying a minimal margin fee on the price.

This margin is called the bid/ask spread and represents the difference between the buy price and the sell price of a stock. This is the same concept that applies when buying foreign currencies while on vacation abroad. You will always get a slightly higher price than what they were bought at. The differential is the price that is paid to the intermediary who offers the purchase and sale prices. These intermediaries are known as market-makers and are responsible for maintaining market liquidity.

The bid/ask differential increases when liquidity decreases and given that it represents a trading cost, which will have to be incurred in addition to the broker costs, it is always worth choosing the most liquid ETF within each category. The fundamental factors of liquidity are:

- The underlying stocks of the ETF - the more highly tradable the better.
- Bottom size - the bigger the better.
- Daily trading volume - the higher the better.
- Market-maker - the more, the better.
- Market conditions - liquidity decreases when markets are highly volatile.

<u>Replication method</u>

How is the index replicated by the ETF? There are three different replication methods.

The total physical replication method is when the ETF holds the same securities as the index, in the same proportion, to offer an accurate performance.

Another type of physical replication is given by sampling. However, in this case the ETF holds a representative sample of the index stocks rather than exactly the same stocks in the same quantities. This method balances the faithful replication of the index with the incurring of high costs that will have to be borne by following an index made up of illiquid and small securities.

The synthetic replication method allows to replicate an index using a total return swap. The swap is a financial instrument that pays the ETF the exact return of the index it hedges. Swaps are usually provided by institutions such as global investment banks, in exchange for money offered by the ETF manager. The synthetic replication method frees the ETF from the obligation of having to physically hold all the index securities. This is very useful especially if the securities of the following index are inaccessible, illiquid or so numerous that it is impossible to hold them.

The synthetic replication method exposes us to counterparty risk, which is the potential inability of the swap provider to meet its commitments.

However, even physical replication can expose us to counterparty risk if the ETF provider takes part in securities lending transactions, or the practice of borrowing securities from other financial operators for the purpose of carrying out a short sale. The stock lending policy of an ETF provider must be posted on that provider's website.

The total replication method is obviously an easier method but it is not always possible for each market.

Use of profits

Distributing ETFs credit income directly to the brokerage account so that it can be spent or reinvested to meet your needs.

Accumulating ETFs do not credit the proceeds but automatically reinvest them in the product itself. In other words, they buy additional shares of the ETF, saving on transaction costs, and increase the value of the investment over time.

Fund location

It is worth knowing where the ETF's registered office is in order to avoid tax complications in the future. Most ETFs are domiciled in Ireland or Luxembourg as these countries offer tax and legal advantages.

ETFs authorized for distribution in Europe are distinguished by the fact that their name contains the acronym UCITS. UCITS is a set of EU regulations that sets standards on counterparty risk, diversification, information disclosure and other forms of consumer protection.

US and Canadian ETFs are not regulated by the UCITS principles and may be subject to additional tax, legal and currency disadvantages. These ETFs are usually distinguished by the fact that there is no UCITS wording in the denomination and their securities identification number (ISIN) starts with US or CA.

Tax situation

Always make sure that your ETF has the fund status subject to the information obligation. This allows you to avoid unpleasant tax shocks in the future. The good news is given by the fact that UCITS ETFs are funds subject to the obligation to inform, but it is always worth doing a quick check in the relevant information sheet.

Currencies

Currency risk is given by the possibility that your foreign investments may be affected by a movement of the dollar. For example, if the dollar strengthens against the euro, stocks quoted in dollars, for European investors who evaluate the performance in euros, will appreciate. Similarly, a weakening of the dollar against the euro means that European investors will enjoy a strengthening of the returns on these same investments. Currency risk tends to smooth out over time and is a major concern for most long-term investors. An exposure to foreign currencies can also offer the opportunity to enjoy the benefits of diversification.

It is known that it is the currency of the ETF's underlyings that determines the currency risk. The S&P 500 ETF exposes you to fluctuations of the dollar value.

If you study and apply these principles, it will be much easier for you to choose the right ETFs for your portfolio.

Chapter 11

Understanding the Features of an ETF from its Name

One of the longest ETF names in the world is UBS ETF (LU) Barclays MSCI US Liquid Corporates Sustainable UCITS ETF (hedged to EUR) A-acc. It is almost an infinite set of terms and abbreviations.

While cryptic names may seem daunting, they usually rely on simple logic that can help you figure out if the ETF is right for you. Once you know how to read the names of the ETFs you will be able to search them more easily.

The keywords may be present in different order or some elements may be missing, but the principle remains.

Let's take a look at some real examples of ETF names to explain the meaning of the keywords.

Issuer

Who issues the ETF? The brand name of the ETF issuer is usually found at the beginning. For example, iShares Core EURO STOXX 50 UCITS ETF. Issuers of ETFs are commonly subsidiaries of large banks or wealth managers. iShares is part of BlackRock, the world's largest wealth manager, while Xtrackers is the brand of Deutsche Bank's ETF and Lyxor belongs to Société Générale.

Base range

The issuer name can also be deciphered by a sub-brand such as Core in the example above. This shows that the ETF is part of a sub-group of a range of the issuer's products. Terms such as Core are worth noting as these products are usually very cheap and generally based on key portfolios such as the EURO STOXX 50 index and MSCI World.

Core and Prime are sometimes used as terms in index names, such as "MSCI USA Prime Vale". In this case, the name has nothing to do with a reference to any particular inexpensive product.

Index

Where do you invest? The second component is the index replicated by the ETF. For example: iShares Core EURO STOXX 50 UCITS ETF.

Well-known index providers include MSCI, FTSE, STOXX and S&P. These provide independent verification of the indexes and licenses them to ETF providers. Often the name of the index reflects the region and the number of stocks followed. For example, the EURO STOXX 50 replicates the 50 largest companies traded in the eurozone.

You may also notice indexes with a suffix such as NR, TR or TRN. NR stands for Net Return, TR stands for Total Return and TRN stands for Total Return Net.

The suffixes tell us whether the index performance is calculated before or after dividend taxes. However, this has no direct impact on the performance of the ETF itself which distributes the dividends due to you.

Regulatory Information Important for Consumer Protection

Always look for the words UCITS in the name of your ETF, as in: iShares Core EURO STOXX 50 UCITS ETF. This abbreviation tells us that the ETF is subject to European regulations specifically designed to protect private investors.

UCITS ETFs must meet certain standards such as not holding more than 20% of the fund's assets in a single financial instrument, in order to facilitate product diversification. The term ETF also represents a regulatory classification. It clearly differentiates ETFs from other exchange-traded products such as ETCs (Exchange Traded Commodities) or ETNs (Exchange Traded Notes).

ETCs and ETNs do not comply with UCITS rules and are subject to additional risks which do not affect ETFs. Before investing in these products make sure you have done thorough research.

Share class

Near the end of the ETF name you will usually find a cryptic abbreviation that provides information on the asset class such as: Xtrackers S&P 500 UCITS ETF 1C.

ETFs often issue different classes of shares. Share classes are variants of the fund that may differ based on fees, trading, currency or return distribution method. You can accurately identify the variant you want from its unique 12-digit ISIN code. Unfortunately, however, each broadcaster uses its own list of abbreviations for this reason it is not possible to decipher it quickly.

The yield paid in the form of dividends or interest can be sent either directly through the brokerage account or automatically reinvested in the ETF in order to increase your share more quickly.

Return paying ETFs are known to be "distributing", such as: iShares FTSE MIB UCITS ETF (Dist). ETFs that reinvest yield are termed "accumulation", such as: iShares FTSE MIB UCITS ETF (Acc).

Distributing ETFs have one of the following abbreviations:

- D
- Dis
- Dist

Accumulation ETFs usually contain one of the following abbreviations:

- C
- Acc

Currency ETFs that invest in eurozone equities carry a currency risk. If the name of the ETF indicates that it is hedged in EUR, this product will be protected against currency fluctuations through the use of forward contracts or options. In the case of Lyxor S&P 500 UCITS ETF Daily Hedged D-EUR, a Euro investor will earn the return of the US index as the hedging will eliminate the effect of the euro's performance against the dollar.

If the currency is known but the term "hedged" is not present, this usually indicates that the ETF is traded in that currency.

Some ETF providers prefer to emphasize the fact that their ETFs are domiciled in Ireland. Why? Because an Irish domicile can offer a tax advantage to some investors. The abbreviation "IE" in UBS ETF names is a great example of this. Be careful when you notice: Short, 2x Leveraged. These risky ETFs allow investors to multiply index movements by a factor of two or three.

ETFs that benefit from falling prices are often referred to as short ETFs.

Be very careful with leveraged products. These are very risky and are specific investments that should only be used by very experienced investors who fully understand how they work.

ETF names are often ambiguous at first glance but you will soon be able to decode them once you master this information.

Conclusion

Congratulations on making it to the end of this book, we hope you found some useful insights to take your stock investing skills to the next level. As you should know by now, the world of stocks is extremely complicated and there is a new "opportunity" every way you look. However, our experience tells us that only by taking things seriously and having a proper plan you can develop your investing skills to the point that you can actually accumulate wealth.

Our final advice is to stay away from the shining objects that the world of stocks offers you every day. Simply dollar cost average into a broad ETF and study the world of stocks in depth. After you have sufficient knowledge on what you are talking about, you can go ahead and invest into single companies. Analyze your results, improve your money management skills and become the master of your emotions.

As you can see, there are no shortcuts you can take. Easy money does not exist. What exists is the possibility to start from zero and work your way up to become a professional stock investor. The journey might be difficult, but it is certainly worth it.

Stock Market Investing Lessons from Real Market Wizards

Learn How to Invest in the Stock Market following the Magic Strategies of Ray Dalio, Bill Ackman and Warren Buffett

By Warren Bell

The following Book is reproduced below with the goal of providing information that is as accurate and reliable as possible. Regardless, purchasing this Book can be seen as consent to the fact that both the publisher and the author of this book are in no way experts on the topics discussed within and that any recommendations or suggestions that are made herein are for entertainment purposes only. Professionals should be consulted as needed prior to undertaking any of the action endorsed herein. This declaration is deemed fair and valid by both the American Bar Association and the Committee of Publishers Association and is legally binding throughout the United States. Furthermore, the transmission, duplication, or reproduction of any of the following work including specific information will be considered an illegal act irrespective of if it is done electronically or in print. This extends to creating a secondary or tertiary copy of the work or a recorded copy and is only allowed with the express written consent from the Publisher. All additional rights reserved. The information in the following pages is broadly considered a truthful and accurate account of facts and as such, any inattention, use, or misuse of the information in question by the reader will render any resulting actions solely under their purview. There are no scenarios in which the publisher or the original author of this work can be in any fashion deemed liable for any hardship or damages that may befall them after undertaking information described herein.

Additionally, the information in the following pages is intended only for informational purposes and should thus be thought of as universal. As befitting its nature, it is presented without assurance regarding its prolonged validity or interim quality. Trademarks that are mentioned are done without written consent and can in no way be considered an endorsement from the trademark holder.

Table of Contents

Introduction

Stocks have taken the world by storm once again after their recovery from the crash of March 2020. After a correction of more than 3 months, the most famous index, the S&P 500 surpassed its previous all time high.

A lot of people are now trying to improvise themselves as professional investors and are losing a lot of money, only helping those who actually know what they are doing accumulate an incredible amount of wealth that will lead to generational fortunes.

To join the club of the few investors that actually make it, you need the right strategies and the right mindset. Notice how we did not include a large initial capital. In fact, while having more money to trade with means having more fire power, it is not necessary to have thousands of dollars to accumulate stocks and build wealth.

In fact, when we started investing in stocks we only had a few hundreds to put into the market, but that sum yielded us thousands and thousands of dollars over the span of a few years.

In this book you are going to discover all the strategies that have allowed us to take investing skills to the next level and everything that helped us understand the stock market. If you diligently apply our advice, we are sure you are going to see amazing results in a relative short period of time, since this market is offering an amazing number of opportunities.

Please, stay away from all the shiny objects of the stock market. Just focus on a few stocks, study them deeply and then milk them like a cash cow. That is the real secret of market wizards!

To your success!

Chapter 1

ETFs and Dividends

As we have seen, investors can choose between ETFs that distribute dividends and ETFs that reinvest them. In this chapter, we will tell you what you need to know to choose between these two types of ETFs.

Let's keep in mind that your goal dictates your strategy. Do you want to generate regular revenue from an existing heritage? Then we suggest you choose ETFs that distribute dividends. Do you want to save money for the future? Then, it will be more appropriate to select ETFs that automatically reinvest the dividends. Meanwhile, many ETF issuers offer both accumulation and distribution ETFs on the same index. But how can you find the ETF that best suits your needs?

Many investors appreciate investments that offer regular revenue distribution, such as real estate investments. It is possible to obtain such investments thanks to specific ETFs.

The dividend revenue are those distributed by profits of equity companies and real estate while interest revenue comes from bond distribution. Investment tools such as gold and raw materials do not provide such revenues.

ETFs dividend revenue is generated when companies distribute part of profits from the index. The ETF collects those dividends and pays them to ETF investors on a regular basis. This could be from one to twelve times a year.

With large global indexes such as the MSCI World, it is possible to obtain a dividend performance of about two percent. In more specialized markets, distributions are sometimes significantly higher. In this way, high-performance ETFs from dividends can be used as a passive yield source.

Almost every bond regularly pays an interest or coupon, which repay creditors in waiting to receive capital return at the end of the period. The greater the risk of default the investor will associate with the issuer, the greater the interest on the bond that the issuer must offer will be.

Given that many nations now require sharing in payments due to the expansive monetary policy and the granting of money, this source of income has moved towards bonds with longer expiry and more risky activity classes.

Use accumulation ETFs for compound interest

in any case, if you decide to save or invest a higher amount of money for future use, accumulation ETFs are the right choice. In this case, the revenue accrued by the composition of the index are automatically reinvested in the ETF in new titles. Therefore, you will not have to worry about reinvesting the proceeds, taking advantage of compound interest and avoiding new commissions that are present when buying new shares of an ETF.

Taxes and ETFs

You must also take into account the differences present in the two types of ETFs regarding their taxation. If you decide to invest in a distribution ETF, dividend or interest revenue you will receive will be taxed at the time of distribution. Therefore the income you receive will be cut by the amount you will have to pay in taxes. On the contrary, ETFs that do not share dividends are not subject to taxation for the proceeds that are reinvested and will be the subject of taxation only when you decide to sell their shares. It is evident that this important difference becomes more significant over time due to the effect of compound interest.

Our favorite strategy is to choose ETFs that do not distribute dividends when you are building your capital and switch to ETFs that distribute them once you are ready to generate a substantial income from your investments.

Chapter 2

Considering the Market Cap

ETFs must have a certain capitalization to be sustainable. Over a certain threshold, ETF profits go up faster than their costs, for this reason the size of the fund is a good indicator of the product duration and its popularity.

Most ETF providers give their new products a year's time to become large enough to become profitable. If after 12 months the ETF is not sustainable, it could be closed.

Advantages of big ETFs

The more the ETF increases the volume of activities under management (AUM), the easier it is to reduce the related spending indicators. This is especially true for the ETFs that replicate market indexes such as the S&P 500 or the MSCI World. The market capitalization of these markets offers the most popular ETFs greater room of maneuver in cost management and incentive to obtain profits. Investors have benefited from the strong competition among ETFs suppliers that contributed to the continuous descent of spending indicators.

The highly capitalized ETFs also tend to have high trading volumes that allow investors to buy and sell more easily, paying lower Bid-Ask spreads, as the market makers can meet demand more easily.

What happens if an ETF is liquidated?

The non-profitable ETFs are closed. It is really a negative event for the investor as it might seem. Therefore, it is worth avoiding it as much as possible.

The positive aspect to remember in this regard is that there are no monetary losses when the ETF is liquidated.

The underlying shares of the ETF still have a market value so you can sell the ETF shares or can wait until the supplier of the ETF does that for you. In any case, at the time of sale you will receive the current net asset value (NAV) of the ETF shares.

Of course you can then reinvest the amount in the market, such as in a more stable ETF of the same category.

However, there are two problems that investors need to face in case of such an event.

First of all, the market can become unfavorable before you are actually able to reinvest the amount. This risk arises in particular if you have to wait for the supplier of the ETF to liquidate the product. Usually there is a delay of about a week before you can actually receive the amount in cash.

Furthermore, if you are forced to liquidate the position you may incur in capital gain tax. This could be the biggest problem, especially if you had planned to hold that investment for a long time. As we will see in the next chapters, every time you need to take money out from your investments, compound interest takes a hit.

Obviously, not all smaller ETFs are at risk of closing. The supplier may decide that certain products can remain niche products and to cover costs with higher spending indexes. However, we do not want you to be in the position of having to liquidate your shares when you do not want it. Therefore, we have created a list of the ETFs with the highest market capitalization.

The 10 larger ETFs (based on the size of the fund)

- iShares Core S & P 500 UCITS ETF (ACC)
- ISHARES CORE MSCI WORLD UCITS ETF USD (ACC)
- Vanguard S & P 500 UCITS ETF

- iShares Core MSCI EMGING Markets IMI UCITS ETF (ACC)
- iShares Core FTSE 100 UCITS ETF (DIST)
- iShares Core S & P 500 UCITS ETF USD (DIST)
- Inveco Physical Gold a
- ISHARES CORE EURO CORPORATE BOND UCITS ETF (DIST)
- Invesco S & P 500 Ucits ETF
- iShares Core DAX UCITS ETF (DE)

Chapter 3

The Impact of Currency Rates

You can easily invest around the world thanks to ETFs. By investing in foreign markets you can improve the performance of your portfolio. However, investing abroad always involves a currency risk. It makes no difference whether you use ETFs or buy single stocks. The increase in terms of value or dividend strategy will not be particularly useful if there is a negative effect of the exchange rate that will reduce the relative yield or make it become negative. There are insurance policies against exchange rate fluctuations, called currency hedged ETFs.

Hedged ETFs

A monetary risk exists when the currency of the country where you invest your money falls or rises against your local currency. For ETFs, you should consider four different currency definitions. Let's take a look at them.

Fund currency

The assets of the ETFs are managed and settled in the fund's currency. All official reports and distributions are also made in the fund's currency. Your bank converts them to the currency in which your account is open. The fund currency for ETFs is generally based on the currency used for the underlying index. The currency of the index is normally the same as the currency where most of the assets traded in the index are included.

Exchange currency

The trading currency determines the currency in which the ETF is traded on a particular market. On the stock markets of Xetra, Milan and Paris, for example, all ETFs are traded exclusively in Euros, regardless of the currency of the ETF fund. Only in the London and Zurich stock exchanges are foreign currencies allowed for trading and you can trade ETFs in different currencies. For you, as an investor, this does not offer any kind of advantage, as any transaction can be instantly converted into any other currency. In addition, you will have to bear additional costs. Exchanging currency plays a very important role for professional players in the market.

Currency of the displayed securities

The values represented in the index represent the ETF's currency risk. Therefore it is important to know which currencies make up the index. If your index contains many foreign currencies, the performance of your investment will be particularly dependent on movements in the exchange rate. In the case of equity securities, the currency is typically equated with the currency of the company's nation - although many international companies are subject to corresponding currency risks. However, companies often reduce their currency risk with currency hedging strategies, as exchange rate fluctuations are not desired by investors or by companies.

Currency hedging of ETFs

Some ETFs are offered with "currency hedge". Hedging can be useful for you to hedge against the impairment of your local currency. Currency hedged ETFs are typically identified by the word "hedge" in the name.

Why do exchange rates fluctuate?

Exchange rates connect the monetary systems of national economies. Goods and capital markets are strongly connected. The exchange rate depends on a number of factors that are not only related to the forex market. Exchange rates, for example, are influenced by the demand for goods and their changes tend to balance supply and demand.

The level of export or import of a nation plays a fundamental role. Nations that import little from abroad but export more are supported in the long run by an increase in exchange rates.

Even the actors in the capital markets are not completely innocent. Interest rates in different markets have their own importance. Large investors are looking for returns and investing money at better interest rates abroad. The exchange rate represents a balance and stops the attractiveness of this type of investment.

Furthermore, central banks influence the value of a currency with an expansionary monetary policy. This policy emerged following the attempt to counter the financial crisis of 2008/2009 and continues to this day in Europe. The greater the amount of money issued, the greater the fall of the local currency against other currencies.

In times of globalization and trade wars, however, such fluctuations are increasing. In most cases, a strong economy dominates smaller nations. Smaller nations can make deals to protect themselves from economic powers.

Other nations, on the other hand, try to keep interest rates constant by setting political goals. China, for example, has a politically controlled interest rate setting system. Another strategy for smaller nations is to make adjustments to monetary reserves. Many emerging markets, for example, issue US dollar bonds. However, in the case of Argentina this led to disastrous consequences and almost national bankruptcy.

The situation is so complex that even economists themselves have difficulty with long-term forecasts. In the short term, banks have developed models that allow hedging and limiting fluctuations. In any case, it is difficult and probably impossible for investors to properly adjust or place bets on exchange rate fluctuations.

Exchange rates represent both an opportunity and a risk for ETF investors

For example, suppose you own EU stocks and the value of the euro falls against the dollar. In this case, your EU shares - calculated in dollars- will lose value, even if the market prices of your euro investments have risen. At the same time, there is of course the probability that the opposite event will occur, that is, an increase in value if the euro strengthens.

This is well illustrated in the MSCI World Index, which covers the stock markets of 23 industrialized nations. The index tracks the global economy in relation to market values, such as market capitalization. The largest capital market in the world, the United States, accounts for the largest weight: more than 60% of the capital in an MSCI World ETF is automatically invested in companies traded in US dollars. Only about more than a tenth of the MSCI World is bought on the eurozone stock markets. The ETF's currency risk for euro zone investors is around

90%, with the US dollar representing the greatest risk. If you live in Switzerland or the UK, the risk is even greater.

How much do currencies contribute to the performance of your ETF?

The influence of exchange rate movements on your ETF investments is present if you make investments outside your currency. Fluctuations in the exchange rate can also redefine an entire investment strategy. For instance, an investment in Chinese government bonds might look attractive following the interest rate above 4% and with a very positive credit rating, but in the past it has offered very low yields for American investors following the development of the exchange rate. If the monetary risk seems to outweigh the opportunity of the return, you should think carefully before investing in an area with a currency different from yours. This includes, for example, emerging market bonds denominated in local currencies.

The period in which to invest in ETFs can be equally decisive. In the short to medium term, favorable exchange rates can be a determining factor in returns. In the long run, however, the situation changes. Economists are increasingly convinced that exchange rates and the development of nations' capital markets will converge in the long run. Therefore, if you invest in the stock markets of large foreign economies over the long term, the exchange rate is already priced in. Furthermore, experts consider it unnecessary to carry out currency hedges for long-term investments.

Chapter 4

The Best ETFs to Invest In

Finally, we can discuss the best ETFs to invest in to beat inflation and build wealth. By now, you should know what an ETF is and why it is the best financial instrument to invest in stocks. But what are the actual ETFs that we recommend? Let's take a look at them in this chapter.

The MSCI World index

The MSCI World index represents a basket made up of over 1,600 international stocks. It is also the objective parameter with which international equity funds are compared.

At a fundamental level, the index is in a neutral zone. If we take into account the fact that over time the index has always risen, albeit undergoing temporary declines, today is still a good time to invest in international equities.

Geographically, the MSCI World sees a predominance of US stocks, which account for 60% of the index thanks to the increases in recent years. The US is followed by Japan with 8.66%, the United Kingdom with 6.33%, France with 3.94% and Germany with 3.46%.

Sectoral analysis

The most important sector is that of technology, which accounts for 18.66% followed by finance which represents 16.73%. Discretionary consumption (12.830%) and the health sector (12%) follow the first two. The limited presence of public utility services makes the index insensitive to interest rate rises.

The MSCI World international stock index allows you to invest in the entire world economy, with the exception of emerging countries.

Index returns and investors returns

In the decade from 2008 to 2018, the compound average annual return of the MSCI World Index in dollars was 7.71% without taking into account dividends and 10.60% taking into account the reinvestment of income.

But what have been the returns obtained by investors over this period of time? We have good reason to believe that the actual gain was much less, perhaps half as much or even less. A first group of investors has lost share trying to beat the market, that is, often entering and exiting the index by buying and selling financial instruments that invest in international equities. The purchase and sale costs and taxes have destroyed the performance obtainable by the investor.

A second group has fallen into the mutual fund trap. Of the 297 products that have at least 10 years of history, 201 have outperformed the MSCI World index without counting dividends. The percentage of "winning" funds in the past is 68%. However, if we take into account dividends, the percentage of funds that beat the index drops to 10%.

Only 31 of the 297 funds available ten years ago managed to generate returns higher than those of the index itself. A real defeat, if you take into account the fact that we have not taken into account the entry fee. The 5% entry fee would have reduced winning funds to 20 out of 297.

It is interesting to note that the index performance difference produced by the reinvestment of dividends is equal to 2.89% per year, about the management cost of international equity funds.

The importance of reinvesting dividends is even more obvious if we consider the fifteen years from January 2000 to December 2015. During this period, the MSCI World index returned 0.75% per annum in dollars. It is no coincidence that there has been talk of a lost decade in the equity markets. Considering the reinvestment of dividends, the yield grows to an average of 3.30% per year.

The performance difference between the two versions of the index stands at 2.55%, an extraordinary similarity with 2.89% in the decade 2008 - 2018.

International equity funds burn the performance of the MSCI World Index by confiscating all dividend income through management costs.

The best Global Equity ETFs on MSCI World

There are several ETFs that allow you to invest in the international stock market. Some of them are more effective, others less. But the choice to use low-cost products instead of traditional actively managed mutual funds turns out to be a winner.

There are many ETFs available on different stock exchanges to invest at low cost in the international stock index. Here is a list of the best one we have found.

- Amundi Msci World - LU1681043599
- Ishares Msci World - IE00B0M62Q58
- Ishares Core Msci World - IE00B4L5Y983
- Ishares Edg Msci Wd Min Volatility - IE00B8FHGS14
- Ishares Msci World Eur Hdg - IE00B441G979
- Lyxor Msci World - FR0010315770
- Xtrackers Msci World - IE00BJ0KDQ92
- Xtrackers Msci World - LU0274208692
- Xtrackers Msci World Eur Hed Swap - LU0659579733

If you want to invest your money in a simple and effective way, just save up 15% of your income each month and buy shares of one of these ETFs. If you take the effect of compound interest into consideration, it is easy to see how this simple action can help you build a fortune.

Chapter 5

Compound Interest

As we have mentioned at the end of the previous chapter, compound interest, combined with a prudent long-term investment, is the secret to accumulating large fortunes. Thanks to the compounding of interests, in fact, it is possible to achieve with relative simplicity - and relatively controlled risks - important financial objectives, as long as you have the right patience. Time is the investor's best friend: starting to invest early, with long time horizons, allows you to position yourself in the best possible way to generate returns.

In this chapter we will explain how compound interest works and how to calculate it. The suggestion for anyone who has the possibility is to start a long-term investment strategy right away.

What is compound interest?

Imagine investing $20,000, earning 10% net interest in one year. This means that at the end of the period you will have generated a capital gain of $2,000. Instead of pocketing these interests, you decide to invest them. Imagine that for the second year your investment again generates 10% interest. The yield is now calculated on a $22,000 basis. This means that your investment will return you $2,200. That is $200 more than it would have returned if you had not reinvested the interest.

Now, a $200 difference isn't particularly significant (considering a 10% return is also relatively high). But let's see what would happen by carrying out the experiment for a long period of time. In the third year, your interest would be calculated on a basis of $24,200, generating a return of $2,420 (instead of the usual $2,000 you would have generated if you had not decided to invest the interest). With the same returns, the extra income that you would have obtained thanks to the reinvestment of interest tends to grow over time, becoming an increasingly large portion of your investment. This is compound interest, an effect that favors investors who decide to remain invested for a long time while also using the returns obtained.

The effect of compound interest, as mentioned, grows exponentially over time. Below you will find a table in which we simulated the result of an investment of $20,000, always imagining an annual return of 10%. In the first column you can see the result by imagining the reinvestment of interest. In the second column you can see the result without reinvesting the interest (simple interest).

Year	Compounding ($)	Not Compounding ($)
1	20,000	20,000
2	22,000	22,000
3	24,200	24,000
4	26,620	26,000

5	29,282	28,000
6	32,210	30,000
7	35,431	32,000
8	38,974	34,000
9	42,872	36,000
10	47,159	38,000
15	75,950	48,000
20	122,318	58,000
25	196,995	68,000
30	317,262	78,000

Simple interest and compound interest

The difference between simple interest and compound interest is quite simple. Simple interest is calculated on the initial capital for each period taken into consideration. For each period (t) the interest is calculated by multiplying the initial capital (C) by the interest accrued for each period. The starting capital always remains the same and constant. On the contrary, in the calculation of compound interest, the interests obtained in the first period (t1) are capitalized, changing the amount of the capital on which the interest will be calculated during the following period (t2).

How is compound interest calculated?

The difference explained in the previous paragraph affects the compound interest calculation formula. With regard to simple interest, the result of an investment (M) is calculated as follows in the case of constant interest:

$$M = C \times (1 + r \times t)$$

The amount is equal to the capital, multiplied by the interest (1+3) for the investment periods. On the contrary, the compound interest formula must take into account the effect of the capitalization of interest and therefore is calculated as follows:

$$M = C \times (1 + r)^t$$

How should the investor behave?

Understanding compound interest brings with it a few important lessons for the investor.

- The earlier you start generating interest, the better the potential long-term result of the investment will be.
- Reinvesting what is obtained thanks to your investment is a choice that can have a huge impact on the result of the investment.
- With the same return, extending the duration of the investment can have exponential effects on the final result.

As you can see, compound interest is your best weapon if you want to invest and have time by your side. We highly recommend you stick with the simple plan of investing a certain amount of money every month in the World Stock Index. It is incredible how wealthy you can become if you do just that. This is the true secret to riches!

Chapter 6

The Right Approach to Compound Interest

The moment you start saving and investing is as important as the amount of money you decide to invest. To truly benefit from the magic of compound interest, it is important to start investing early. Earnings generate earnings, which in turn generate even greater earnings.

For this reason, we should start investing as soon as we have some savings available, whether they are the first salaries after graduation or even better the result of some extraordinary work during the studies.

Here are some simple tips for those who decide to start this path.

Prepare for a marathon, not a sprint.

Once you have entered the world of work, the tendency is to relate competitively with your peers: you are confronted with who has obtained the most profitable job, who has bought a house first and so on. In reality these comparisons are not predictive: those who start the race at a faster pace do not always win the marathon in the long run.

And in any case, developing confrontation with the people we think are doing better than us is not helping our financial well-being, according to research from Morningstar.

Following a survey of several hundred people, the study concludes that "frequent comparisons are associated with greater financial stress, less satisfaction, lower savings and overall more negative feelings about one's financial life".

Instead, the research concluded that respondents with a financial role model were more likely to feel confident in their ability to achieve their financial goals. Hence, one of the best actions you can take as an investor is to find a financial mentor.

Start investing for the long term

As a recent graduate, you may be surprised at how little is needed to start investing - and how much these first investments can generate additional wealth.

An initial investment of $1,000 with an additional $100 of investments every month for 40 years, at a not unreasonable rate of return of 7%, would be enough to reach up to $280,000.

Investing in the long term is essential but it is equally important to set expectations.

Most investments and stocks in particular can have large returns but equally important fluctuations over time. Predicting the returns of an investment in the short term is a rather difficult exercise, so it is important to think over a longer period of time and be prepared to withstand fluctuations, sometimes even substantial, in your portfolio.

Always keep an emergency fund

Even if you started very early and you are aware that the time horizon of your investments is long-term, you will still need to insure against extraordinary events that can change your plan during the course.

Therefore, consider purchasing health and disability insurance. And at every stage of life it is vital to build at least a small financial cushion to cover unexpected expenses.

The common rule of thumb is that you should have three to six months of expenses set aside in extremely liquid investments like an online savings account. Of course, if you are young and have just started earning, this figure can seem huge and disproportionate.

However, remember that the emergency fund is intended to cover basic expenses: housing costs, insurance costs, public services and food. From this point of view, accumulating excess cash as a buffer is a more than sensible solution.

Investing in human capital before life gets complicated

We talk too little about it when it comes to investing, but remember that one of the best investments you can make is in yourself. Human capital is just as important as money capital. After all, your income will probably depend on the job you have and therefore on your level of education and preparation.

Secondly, remember that knowledge is an asset that no one can ever take away from you. Therefore carefully consider the trade off between focusing exclusively on the work that guarantees you your current income or dedicating periods of your life to expanding your professional training and not that they can be the springboard for future leaps forward.

The previous points take into consideration the importance of decisions when it comes to resource allocation. Harnessing the long-term potential of human capital by investing in additional education and exploiting the long-term return potential of equities, guiding our money investment decisions.

But there is a decision on the allocation of resources that is the most important of all: the allocation over time. All of us in one way or another try to balance the time spent earning money with that spent doing things that bring us joy or that are good for us.

In the end, the optimal allocation of time is strictly personal and can change over the course of everyone's life. The best advice on this front is simply to say that, unlike investing in ETFs, the allocation of time is deserves frequent and constant monitoring.

Chapter 7

DCA: The Best Investing Strategy

Many savers, even in times of crisis, are wondering what are the advantages of dollar cost averaging plans, the risks and the actual costs.

The dollar cost averaging plan is often defined as one of the best ways for the saver to invest in the financial markets. Those who have only a few hundred dollars a month to invest may find it too risky to expose themselves independently to the markets. Instead, the accumulation plan allows you to invest in a mutual fund or ETF through the payment of installments.

What is dollar cost averaging?

Let's start from the basics. A dollar cost averaging plan is a way of investing in one or more financial instruments on a regular basis.

In doing so, the investor does not necessarily have to be in possession of large capital to enter the financial markets, but can pay a monthly sum to those who invest for him.

The characteristics that describe the basics of the dollar cost averaging plan are as follows.

- the saver invests constant amounts;
- the payment of the shares takes place regularly;
- the duration can be decided on the go;

Dollar cost averaging plans are created to appeal to all types of savers, especially those who, despite the lack of liquidity available, still want to invest in the stock and bond markets. An essential factor in investing using a dollar cost averaging plan is the constancy factor: the investment is made constantly and continuously.

To meet the most diverse needs of the saver, it is possible to customize in detail the dollar cost averaging plan.

How it works

Through a dollar cost averaging plan, the investor is given the opportunity to invest a constant sum through regular payments for the agreed duration with the aim of subscribing to financial instruments and earning thanks to the increase in their value. Instead of investing the entire sum immediately, the saver gradually invests an amount that increases over time.

The total value of the investment is given by multiplying the amount of the monthly investment by the number of months. To better understand this concept and how a dollar cost averaging plan works, let's make an example.

The investor chooses to invest 150 dollars for 180 months (15 years). At the end of the term of the dollar cost averaging plan, the investor will be able to boast a capital of 27,000 dollars in total, to which the appreciation must be added.

The duration of the dollar cost averaging plan

The duration of a dollar cost averaging plan follows the constraint of a minimum duration set at one year while the maximum may vary from the fund to which it is used, in any case up to a maximum of 40 years. The number and frequency of the basic investment installments is monthly but the annual commitment can be reduced to a smaller number of installments (bi-monthly, quarterly, quarterly, half-yearly) up to a single installment per year. We suggest you invest on a monthly basis.

The advantages of dollar cost averaging

Among the advantages of investing through a dollar cost averaging plan we find the following.

- Flexibility. The investor is in control of the duration of the investment.
- Small payments. The investors with low financial resources can also invest in a dollar cost averaging plan.
- Seasonality risk reduced. Thanks to a regular investment frequency it is possible to eliminate seasonality and sudden fluctuations on the markets.

- Constant savings. Through the dollar cost averaging plan, the investment is automated and constant, reducing the risk of spending your savings in a less fruitful way.

- Zero emotions. Through a dollar cost averaging plan the possibility that the investor acts at the mercy of emotions is eliminated.

This investment strategy rose to prominence in the 1950s thanks to the man who is considered the father of fundamental analysis: Benjamin Graham. According to the investor, who also admitted to being inspired by the well-known Warren Buffet, following this technique is advisable to have a greater splitting of the amounts to invest, and a high diversification of the companies on which to bet on.

We can only support Graham's view and we think that a dollar cost averaging plan is the best solution for most investors.

Chapter 8

Investing in Single Stocks: the Basics

Some of you might be interested in investing in single stocks, even if we recommend a simple dollar cost averaging plan with a monthly purchase of one or two ETFs. This is why we have decided to dedicate the next chapters at a practice called "stock picking". This is the art and science of finding interesting stocks to invest in.

What aspects should you pay attention to when evaluating a stock? The so-called indicators will help you in this operation. The indicators that, at first glance, may seem difficult and complex to calculate will allow you to quickly discover interesting aspects of a company by going a little deeper into the topic.

Indicators provide you with important information to make a comparison between stocks and opt for a particular investment. Below we present the five main indicators .

The price/earning ratio

The Price / Earnings Ratio (P/E) or ratio is probably the most important indicator for evaluating stocks. It is calculated with a very simple formula: "share price" divided by "share profit". Here is an example of a calculation: the current price of a stock is $100 per share. Last year, a profit of $5 per share was achieved. For the profit, the value forecast by analysts for the current financial year is generally applied. In our example, the P / E therefore amounts to 100 divided by 5 = 20. In other words, the P / E indicates how many times the profit is contained in the current price of a stock, or after how many years the profit has "paid off" the share.

The lower the P / E is, the better the valuation of a share and the higher the expected company profit for the future. The P / E is only suitable for comparing similar business models to each other. In any case, it must be clarified precisely why a P / E is low or high. As an indication, it is interesting to know that in 2017 the P / E of all securities listed in the NYSE amounted on average to 24.6.

The price / book value ratio

The Price / Book Value (P / B), or the relationship between price and book value, is obtained by dividing the price of a share by the book value per share. The book value per share, which corresponds to the equity per share resulting from the balance sheet of a company, is generally lower than the current market value. Here is an example of a calculation: if a company has a book value of $5 billion and has 200 million shares in circulation, the resulting book value per share is $25. If the listing of this company amounts to $30 per share, the P / B is equal to 1.2.

If the P / B per share is less than one, this effectively means that the company on the stock exchange is worth less than all the machinery, stocks and properties grouped together. In fact, this is a clear signal for a profitable purchase. But beware: there are different methods of budgeting and valuation, and the P / B provides little guidance for companies with high intangible values. Real estate can also be included in the book value in different ways. The P / B varies a lot according to the sector and can be easily "manipulated". Therefore there is not even a general rule to evaluate it.

The dividend yield

To calculate the dividend yield, divide the dividend by the current share price and multiply it by 100. It indicates the return on invested capital per share as a percentage. Here is an example of a calculation: if the dividend of a share is equal to $10 and the price at $200 the resulting dividend yield is 5%. The higher the dividend yield, the better. Here too, however, an important clarification must be made: a high return can also result from a low share price, which may indicate a lack of interest from investors or that the company makes payments that are too high that are not covered by the profits.

Return on equity

The return on equity indicates the relationship between equity and the profit of a company, or the remuneration of the capital employed. This indicator allows you to establish whether a company achieves high profits with little money and therefore has a more or less high profitability. A high return on equity is better than a low one. Here is an example of a calculation: a company totals $250,000 in profits. The equity capital amounts to $4 million. The return on equity is equal to 250,000: 4,000,000 x 100 = 6.25%. Also in this case, the different possibilities for setting up accounts, and consequently the way in which the company calculates its equity, can constitute potential traps. The return on equity can increase, in fact, even with the acquisition of third party capital and optimize the result.

Profit growth

The profit growth indicates the percentage increase in the profit of each share from one financial year to the next. This indicator helps to avoid the purchase of shares of a company with stagnant or declining profits. By comparing the profit growth again with the P / E indicated above, the PEG (Price / Earnings to Growth Ratio) is obtained. For example, if the P / E amounts to 20 and the estimated future earnings growth of 20%, the resulting PEG is equal to 1. A value of 1 is generally considered a fair valuation. Shares with a PEG below 1 are underestimated.

The five indicators described above are the main and most frequent parameters for valuing stocks. However, you will notice that there are always some doubts and unknown variables. Furthermore, it is not always easy to identify a reasonable comparison for the indicator. We invite you to carry out careful research, study the annual closures and compare companies within the sector and with benchmarks. The more you know about a company and its financial situation, the more complete the resulting stock valuation picture will be.

Chapter 9

Balance Sheets

It is a document that takes a snapshot of the company's assets at a given moment, comparing assets and liabilities. In order to carry out its business, the company needs assets that it must finance through the use of shareholder capital or third party capital. Through the balance sheet it is possible to identify which investments are made by the company and how they have been financed.

In the balance sheet, both assets and liabilities are divided respectively into current assets and current liabilities. This division helps the investor to better understand the financial situation of the company. Put simply, current assets are those that follow the cash conversion cycle. This means that they are transformed from money into commodities, then from commodities into credits, and then back into cash credits. Generally, if an asset is expected to be transformed into cash within 12 months it is accounted for as "current".

Similarly, a liability is current when it is expected to be paid within the following 12 months. Beyond the classification and the underlying criteria, it is important for the investor to analyze each category, asking himself why the numbers are like this and what could possibly make them change in the future.
Here are some questions that obviously do not intend to represent an exhaustive list, rather a starting point for developing a critical attitude aimed at understanding the "story" that the numbers tell.

Cash and cash equivalents

Are they bank accounts? If so, are they held in bankruptcy banks? Are they held in currencies at risk of devaluation? If they are short-term securities, what type of securities are they and what risk do they present?

Receivables from customers

Who are they and where are the customers? Are they at risk of bankruptcy or partial insolvency? Do they have a history of on-time payments in the past? Is the write-down recorded in the financial statements for impaired loans congruent with their presumed realizable value? Are they denominated in a currency at risk of devaluation?

Warehouse inventories

What types of inventories are they? With what criteria are they evaluated? Are they still salable goods or that no one wants anymore?

Tangible fixed assets

What do they consist of? Is their real value lower or higher than what is reported in the financial statements? Are there any fixed assets already depreciated at 100% but still in use?

Intangible assets

With what criteria were they evaluated? Do trademarks and/or patents have a presumable value in line with that reported? What could make this value change? Are there any fixed assets already 100% depreciated but still in use?

Financial fixed assets

Are they valued at purchase cost or market value? If these are investments in other companies, how are they valued?

Payables to banks and long-term loans

When is the payment of these debts expected? Will there be enough liquidity on that date to be able to pay? If it were necessary to refinance the debt, at what interest rate would it be possible to do so? And what effect would the new interest rate have on the company's profits?

Payables to suppliers and to the tax authorities

When do they need to be paid? And what obstacles are there to a possible deferral of payment?

Provisions for risks

What kind of risks do they refer to? What evaluation criteria were used? Are these funds fair to the risks or are they underestimated?

Another important aspect to evaluate concerns the synchronization between the deadlines of the uses and the sources, in particular we are talking about:

- Investments in fixed assets should tend to be financed by durable loans (equity + consolidated liabilities)
- The balance between current assets and short-term liabilities, on the other hand, guarantees the correlation of income - expenditure

Starting from the balance sheet it is possible to build some indicators that help us to analyze the financial and equity structure of the company. Here we report only a couple of them by way of example, recalling once again that from the investor's point of view, the theoretical approach is less important than the practical one aimed at understanding the numbers.

Debt indicator

Measuring the incidence of third party assets on total liabilities is used to express an opinion on the degree of capitalization of the company.

Quick Ratio

It measures the ratio between the capital in circulation excluding the warehouse and the total current liabilities. It expresses the ability to meet short-term debts using short-term availability, without considering inventories which, as regards the safety stock, are more fixed assets than current assets.

Chapter 10

The Relationship Between the Balance Sheet and the Income Statement

As we have said in the previous chapter, the balance sheet is a snapshot of the situation of a company at a given moment, while the income statement shows what happened to it in a previous period.

The balance sheet says that, today, the company has certain characteristics while the income statement says how much money the company has earned (or lost) in the previous period. The two documents are therefore closely related. In fact, it is thanks to what happened last year that the company has the characteristics it has today. Once again, using some simplifications, we can say that the balance sheet is determined by the income statement.

For the calculation of the profitability indicators we will use a representation scheme of the balance sheet and a reclassified income statement which allows us to isolate the generators of company profitability by identifying the return on invested capital and that of shareholders' equity.

The return on invested capital (before tax) can be defined as the ratio between Operating Result (or EBIT) and the invested capital and is expressed by an indicator called ROI (Return On Investment). This ratio indicates the profitability of the characteristic management of the company, regardless of the effects of the financing policies and extraordinary management and before taxes. The same ratio calculated, however, net of notional taxes is called ROIC (Return On Invested Capital)

The return on equity can be defined as the ratio between net profit and equity and is expressed by an index called ROE (Return On Equity).

The connection between the 2 indicators can be expressed through a financial relationship that summarizes the contribution of various factors to ROE, distinguishing 3 growth drivers:

- Operating profitability after tax (called ROIC)
- Financial leverage (net debt / equity ratio), given by the ratio between net financial position and shareholders' equity
- The difference between operating profitability and the average cost of debt (calculated as the ratio between financial charges and net debt), net of taxes.

The choice to finance the net invested capital through debt influences the ROE. If a company finances its business only with its own capital, the ROE obviously coincides with the ROI after taxes. When the debt grows, the difference between ROE and ROI is determined by the financial leverage (D/E) and by the difference between ROI and the cost of debt.

Obviously the overall profitability of the company (expressed by ROE) will be greater than the operating profitability if the company is able to borrow at a rate lower than that of the operating profitability and this effect will be amplified the greater the degree of debt of the company.

The use of financial leverage, which under certain conditions makes the use of debt convenient, at the same time determines an increase in the riskiness of the investment. In fact, a crisis could suddenly deteriorate the company's margins and thus reverse the spread between ROIC and cost of debt (ROIC <Cost of debt). At that point the use of leverage would amplify the effect of destruction of value. Intuitively, the company would find itself in a situation in which it obtains a lower return from the borrowed capital than the interest it has to pay on it, thus eroding the return on shareholder capital.

Chapter 11

Cash Flow Analysis

The cash flow, not to be confused with the profit for the year, is the amount of net financial resources produced by the company in a year. It is the difference between all revenues and all outputs generated.

The profit for the year, on the other hand, is the difference between revenues and costs incurred in the year, regardless of the actual collection of revenues for the invoices issued and the actual payment of costs for the invoices received.

In an ideal economic world in which there are no deferrals in receipts from customers and deferred payments to suppliers, there would be perfect or almost coincidence between the profit for the year and the money that remains with the company at the end of the year.

Since we are not in an ideal business world, there are delays granted to customers to pay their revenue bills. The suppliers in turn grant deferrals in payments for cost invoices. For many companies there is also the warehouse of raw materials and products that must be purchased for operational activity and which determine differences between cash flow and operating profit.

Basically, whenever a company grants credit to customers, it is implicitly financing them, absorbing financial resources that are subtracted from other needs, such as the payment of salaries, taxes and suppliers. For the purposes of evaluating an investment, we can say that the most important aspect of a company is its ability to generate cash flows and not accounting profits. After all, as the saying goes: "cash is king". Therefore, let's take a closer look at the document that highlights the company's cash flow in a given period.

The financial statement measures the sources of liquidity of a company and its uses of cash for a specific period of time. The net cash flow is determined by three different types of cash flows, which in turn can be calculated as the algebraic sum of balance sheet values and / or income statement:

- Cash flow from operating activities
- Cash flow from investing activities
- Cash flow from financial activities

From a technical point of view, the cash flow statement can be prepared using two methods.

- Indirect method Starting from the economic result, the changes of a financial nature that have had an impact on company liquidity are reconstructed "backwards".
- Direct method. From the operations that gave rise to cash receipts (sales revenues, interest income, etc.), the operations that gave rise to cash outflows are subtracted (purchase of materials and goods, services, personnel, passive, etc.).

In company financial statements, the analysis of flows is usually presented with the indirect method only.

In order to provide a more complete judgment on the ability of a company to generate cash flows, it is appropriate to contextualize the analysis with the phases of the company's life cycle and in particular with the investment cycle of the company and the sector in which it operates.

In the early stages of development, cash flows can be negative in spite of significant investments aimed at building production capacity to meet future demand. Moving towards the stage of maturity, cash flows will increase as a consequence of the increase in revenues and profits while investments in production capacity will decrease with a consequent and further increase in cash generation.

If we put ourselves in the perspective of who has to invest in a company, we will have to take into consideration what is called Free Cash Flow to the Firm (FCFF). This is the cash flow generated by the operating activity (and net of Capex) available to remunerate all investors, be they shareholders or bondholders.

FCFF = Operating cash flow - Capex (reinvestment needs)

Since the FCFF represents the cash flow available to meet the needs of all the company's investors, it will be used (as we will see in the next posts) to determine the overall value of the company (Equity + Debt).

If, on the other hand, we wanted to evaluate only the company's net capital (Equity), we would have to consider a different cash flow, defined as Free Cash Flow to Equity (FCFE). This is the cash flow available only to shareholders, which remains after that both taxes and financial charges for the remuneration of capital lenders have been deducted.

Chapter 12

Discounted Cash Flow

As we mentioned in the previous chapter, the idea behind the valuation method that takes into account cash flows is that the value of each asset can be considered as dependent on 3 variables.

- The cash flows generated by it
- The time horizon of their manifestation
- Their riskiness

The more precisely the 3 variables can be determined, the simpler and more specific the evaluation can be. This method is based on two simple considerations: it is better to have $10 today rather than in the future;

therefore it is better a less risky flow than a more risky one if the amount is the same.

For example, suppose we need to value an asset consisting of a bond that does not pay periodic coupons but guarantees the payment of a nominal value of $102 in one year.

In this case, 2 of the 3 variables are precisely determined: the time horizon of 1 year and the amount of guaranteed cash flow in 12 months ($102). Let us assume, once again in theory, that this asset is risk-free and that the rate associated with a risk-free investment with the same characteristics is 2%. In this case we have also determined the third variable.

By applying the DCF ("Discounted cash Flow") method, to obtain the value of our asset we will discount the cash flows ($102) for the rate that reflects the risk (2%). In other words we will calculate the equivalent value to date of the cash flow that we will be able to obtain from our asset in a year.

The mathematical calculation is quite simple: 102 $ / (1 + 2%) or 102 $ / 1.02 which gives us as a result $100.

We deliberately presented the simplest case represented by an asset with certain cash flows, without risk and with a defined time horizon. In the real world, as investors, we will also find ourselves having to evaluate assets that face different types of risk including the following.

- "Default Risk". This is when assets with certain cash flows have a risk of default (eg bonds). In this case it is necessary to translate the default risk into a spread to be applied at the risk-free rate to discount the cash flows.

- "Equity Risk". This is when assets do not have secure cash flows. In this case it is necessary to address 2 fundamental points: how to measure these cash flows and how to estimate their expected level.

As we have repeated several times, when we buy a share we are buying a "piece" of a company and its business. In estimating cash flows, we will then have to ask ourselves if we want to evaluate the company as a whole or just its equity.

The company, in fact, can be seen as a set of activities, financed partly with debt and partly with equity. Similarly, the cash flows produced by the company will be used to remunerate all investors in it, shareholders and non-shareholders.

If we evaluate the company from the shareholder's point of view, the cash flows that we will have to consider will be only those that remain after all operating costs, taxes and financial charges have been deducted: we define this flow as cash flow available for shareholders. These cash flows will be discounted at a rate that reflects their riskiness and which we define as the Cost of Equity.

If we decide to evaluate the company as a whole, we will use a broader cash flow concept that measures the cash flow generated by the operating activity and intended to remunerate all investors, shareholders and non-shareholders. This is the cash flow available to investors. The discount rate of these flows will obviously be a weighted average between the cost of equity and the cost of debt capital. This rate is defined as the Cost of Capital.

It is very important to remember the consistency between the cash flows examined and the relative discount rate: the cash flows for the shareholders must be discounted at the cost of equity, while the cash flows available for investors at the cost of capital.

Chapter 13

Stay Away from Leverage

Through the use of financial leverage a person has the possibility to buy or sell financial assets for an amount greater than the capital owned and, consequently, to benefit from a potential return greater than that deriving from a direct investment in the underlying asset. However, investors expose themselves to the risk of very significant losses.

Let's see how the concept of leverage works starting from a simple case. Let's assume we have $100 available to invest in a security.

Let's assume that the expectations of gain or loss are equal to 30%: if things go well, we will have $130, otherwise, we will have $70. This is a simple speculation where we bet on a certain event.

In the event that we decide to risk more by investing, in addition to our $ 100, another $900 borrowed, the investment would take on a different articulation since we use a leverage of 10 to 1. If things go well and the stock rises by 30%, we would receive$1300. We would return the $900 borrowed with a profit of $300 on an initial capital of 100. We would obtain a profit of 300% with a stock that in itself gave a 30% yield. Obviously we will have to pay interest on the $900 borrowed, but the general principle remains valid: leverage allows you to increase possible earnings.

Considering the further case of investing in derivatives. Let's say we buy a derivative that, in a month, gives the right to buy 100 grams of gold at a price set today of $5,000. We could physically buy gold with an outlay of$5,000 and keep it waiting for the price to go up and then sell it back. If we decide to use derivatives, we should not have $5,000, but only the capital necessary to buy the derivative. Let's say that a bank sells the derivative for $100 that allows us to buy the same 100 grams of gold for $5,000 in a month. If in a month gold is worth $5,500, we can buy and sell it immediately, making a profit of $500. Not counting the $100 price of the derivative, we make a profit of $400 with $100. That is a 400% return.

Without using derivatives and leverage, the same $500 could have been earned only for an investment of $5,000, making a profit of 10%.

The potential of using leverage is clear. But be careful: the multiplier effect of financial leverage, described with the previous examples, also works if the investment goes wrong. For example, in the event that we decide to invest $100 in our possession plus an additional sum of $900 borrowed, if the stock depreciates by 30%, we would be left with only $700 in hand; having to repay the $900 borrowed plus interest and considering the $100 of our initial investment we would have a loss of over $300 on an initial capital of$200. In percentage terms, the loss would be 300% compared to a decrease in the value of the stock of 30%.

Another element to keep in mind is that the various financial levers can be accumulated: in this way speculation operations are carried out using a "squared financial leverage" with evident repercussions on possible outcomes.

What may seem like an interesting instrument with positive potential for the investor, on the other hand, presents risks that must be taken into consideration. Indeed, if the financial system as a whole works with very high leverage and financial institutions lend money to each other to multiply their possible profits, the loss of a single investor can trigger a domino effect, infecting the entire financial market.

Banks are typically subjects that operate with a more or less high degree of financial leverage: for a given net capital, the total of assets in which the resources are invested is generally much higher. For example, a bank with equity of $100 and leverage of 20 manages assets for $2,000. A loss of 1% of the assets results in the loss of 20% of the equity.

The development of the market for the transfer of credit risk (from financial intermediaries to the market) has meant that the traditional bank model, known as "originate-and-hold", has been replaced for many operators by the "originate-to-distribute" one, with the effect of a further increase in financial leverage. The spread of this second banking model is one of the factors that explain the crisis that has started in the subprime mortgage market.

Inflation in real estate prices has supported the issuance of securitized loans and the exponential development of the related market, allowing banks to make huge profits and, at the same time, increase leverage. But "the money machine" could not last long and eventually many banks found themselves without sufficient capital to absorb the losses resulting from the turnaround in the housing market, effectively resulting in bankruptcy companies.

In the meantime, the example of banks has spread within the financial system, spreading to all other financial institutions. Financial leverage had taken over, especially in the United States, generating a huge volume of risky investments that rested on a fraction of share capital. Think of the issuance of so-called "credit default swaps" (derivative instruments used to hedge against the risk of default of the debtor): some insurance companies were heavily exposed to the real estate market and when the latter collapsed and the value of mortgages fell, they began to lose without having sufficient capital to absorb the losses resulting from the issuance of those instruments.

In order not to risk bankruptcy and return to sufficient bank capital levels, it is possible to resort to capital increases. This is done through the reduction of the amount of loans to businesses and the disposal of other liquid assets. The result of all this in the period of the outbreak of the subprime crisis was a credit freeze and a crash in the stock market. These are the main channels through which the financial crisis hit the real economy. Credit rationing has affected investments and the decline in the stock market has reduced the value of household wealth and of consumption.

We know that a certain level of leverage is physiological to support economic growth, even if we have no indication of what the optimal level is. However, history teaches us how in an increasingly globalized and interdependent economic-financial system, financial leverage can be a trigger for speculative bubbles. And it is in these periods that the strongest disconnect between finance and the real economy is generated.

Please, stay away from leveraged products. They are only good to make you lose all your capital. As Bill Ackman once said, 10% a year is all you need to build a fortune.

Chapter 14

A Lesson from Warren Buffett

Born in 1930 in Omaha,Nebraska, Warren Buffett is the second of three children of a member of the United States Congress, Howard Buffett. He began his education at Rose Hill Elementary School in Omaha.

In 1942 his father was elected to the United States Congress and after moving with his family to Washington DC, Warren finished elementary school. After that, he attended Alice Deal Junior High School, eventually earning a master's degree to Columbia Business School, the university where his idol Benjamin Graham taught. Benjamin Graham is the author of the well-known book "The intelligent investor".

Warren Buffett devoted himself to equity investments from a very young age; legend has it that he started investing at the age of 11, using the savings obtained by selling drinks bought in his paternal grandfather's shop at school. There is also a report of a plot of land bought at the age of 14 and rented by him to local shepherds. After graduation, he accepted Graham's own invitation to work in New York for Graham-Newman Corp., considered by many to be the first true hedge fund in history. In 1955 Graham retired and offered him the position of partner of the company, but Buffett decided to refuse and return to his hometown. With the capital available to him, he believed to be able to live easily on an income thanks to his investment skills. But back in Omaha, friends and relatives asked him to manage their money.

So, almost by chance, he founded the Buffett Partnership, an investment fund with which he applies the investment strategies taught by Benjamin Graham. These strategies fall under the umbrella of value investing, that is, the search for undervalued stocks to buy and hold for very long periods. Through this investment method, Buffett acquired important stakes in giants such as Coca Cola, Gillette, McDonald's, Kirby Company and Walt Disney. Subsequently, he decided to go public on the Buffett Partnership by merging it with a listed textile company, Berkshire Hathaway. According to the Condé Nast ranking he was the sixteenth best manager of all time.

Berkshire Hathaway

His high-level financial activity began in 1962, the year in which he began to acquire shares in Berkshire Hathaway, a declining textile industry, of which he would take control a few years later. With Berkshire Hathaway, flanked by partner Charlie Munger, he began to buy undervalued companies in the most varied sectors, from services to industry, from insurance to private jets; finally, it acquired Mid American Holding, active in the energy sector, and thus began to invest in pipe factories.

The insurance sector

With Berkshire Hathaway, he acquired two insurance companies in 1967: the National Fire and Marine Insurance Company and the National Indemnity Company. The insurance sector conquers more and more space within the Buffett holding. Since 1985 the company has definitively abandoned the textile sector to devote itself exclusively to the insurance sector. Today Berkshire Hathaway is the largest reinsurer in the world after the Swiss Swiss Re and the German Munich Re; since 2018 it has been the main shareholder of Cattolica Assicurazioni.

Philanthropy

In 2006 Buffett donated $37 billion in charitable actions for people of the Third World. In June 2006, he announced a plan to donate his fortune to charity, 83% in favor of the Bill & Melinda Gates Foundation.

He also pledged to donate the equivalent of approximately 10 million Berkshire Hathaway class B shares to the Bill & Melinda Gates Foundation, worth approximately $30 billion. It is the largest donation in history, and makes Buffett one of the leaders of capitalist philanthropism. The foundation will receive 5% of the total donation on an annual basis in July of each year, starting from 2006. As you can see, the commitment to the foundation is significant with the commitment to donate. Every year, starting from 2009 , an amount that is at least equal to the value of the previous year's contribution, plus 5% of the foundation's net assets is donated. Buffett also joined the board of directors of the Gates Foundation, although to this day he has no intention of actively participating in their investments.

An investing lesson from Warren

Buffett uses several methods to evaluate the share price, including sophisticated and detailed analysis of the various operations of a company.

The first method he used is to analyze the initial rate of return and its value with respect to government bonds, taking the figure for earnings per share for each year and dividing it by the long-term interest rate of government bonds.

For example, in 1994 Buffett began buying stock in Gannett Corp., a newspaper holding company. Earnings per share that year were estimated at $3.20 per year, government bonds had a yield of 7%. Dividing $3.20 by 7% yields a relative value of $45.71 per share. In other words, if you paid $45.71 for Gannett, you would have an initial yield equal to that of government bonds. Paying a higher price would result in a lower initial yield than government bonds. In fact if you paid $50 the initial yield would be $3.20/$50, or 6.4%. However, earnings per share grow every year so the initial yield would also grow. Would you rather invest $45.71 in government bonds and earn a static 7% or would you rather invest the same amount in stocks and get an initial 7% profit but a higher return in subsequent years based on an increase in earnings per share? The answer for Warren Buffett was pretty simple.

Another method used by Buffett is to project the compound index of return based on historical gains in earnings per share.

For example, earnings per share at Gannett had grown at a compound annual rate of return of 8.6% in the ten years prior to the purchase of Buffett. If the earnings per share of $3.20 in 1994 had grown annually, for the ten consecutive years, at an annual rate corresponding to the historical one, the earnings per share in the tenth year would have been $7.30.

These estimated earnings per share can be multiplied by the medium high and medium low ratio of the p/e per share ratio over the past ten years to provide an estimate of price change in the tenth year.

If profits are redistributed, an estimate of the amount of dividends paid over the ten years must also be added to the 10-year prices.

Once the future prices have been established, the performance indicators over the next ten years must be determined based on the current selling price of the share. Buffett requires a return of at least 15% to make an investment. Buffett takes advantage of "good deals". For example, when a bear market drives prices down or if an unfavorable view of the market in the short term causes the price of a stock to fall. However, his valuation focuses on earnings growth and is not averse to buying stocks at a higher valuation if he is confident in earnings expansion.

Buffett is not conducive to great diversification, as it is difficult to sufficiently analyze and understand a large number of companies. Furthermore, it does not diversify the portfolio based on the choice of sectors. In reality, his choice to avoid commodity based companies leads to the exclusion of certain groups. Instead, Buffett's method to control risk within the portfolio involves some fundamental points.

- be sure that the investment was made in an expanding company;
- accurately understand and analyze the nature of companies;
- be sure to pay a reasonable price for the shares.

Buffett is also a long-term investor, and some of the companies he has chosen have remained in his portfolio for over 20 years. While his mentor, Benjamin Graham, favors a sale when the stock price reaches its intrinsic value, Buffett continues to hold it until the company's growth potential is better than alternative investments.

According to Buffett, you should definitely not sell if you have bought the shares of an excellent company that is growing consistently and that has quality management that works in the interest of the shareholders. If these circumstances changed - the nature of the company or its management, then Buffett would sell. Or it would sell if an alternative investment offered a better return.

Chapter 15

A Lesson from Ray Dalio

Raymond Dalio was born in the neighborhood of Jackson Heights, in the borough of Queens, New York City. He is the only child of an Italian-American jazz musician, Marino Dallolio (1911-2002), who "played the clarinet and saxophone in Manhattan jazz clubs like the Copacabana", and Ann, a housewife. He grew up on Long Island where he attended a public school. He invested in the stock market at just 12 years old, buying Northeast Airlines shares for $300 and tripling the investment after the airline merged with another company. At 18, he already had a stock portfolio worth a few thousand dollars.

He graduated in finance from Long Island University, then took an MBA from Harvard Business School. He started working in a brokerage firm from where he was fired for punching his boss in the face. Then, Ray dealt with commodities at Dominick & Dominick LLC. In 1974 he was a futures broker at Shearson Hayden Stone.

In 1975 he founded Bridgewater Associates in his two-bedroom apartment in Manhattan, an investment management company focusing more on riskier asset classes. In 1981 he opened an office in Westport, Connecticut. Four years later, in 1985, Ray went to China for the first time and was fascinated by it to the point of returning often and studying deeply the Chinese system and culture.

In 2005 the company, which operated on all financial markets, from gold to yen, using quantitative analysis and algorithms, was among the largest hedge funds in the world with assets under management. In 2007 Bridgewater predicted in advance the financial crisis that broke out in 2008 due to problems related to the mortgage market; it was one of the few companies that made money as the world was collapsing. Also in 2008 Dalio published an essay explaining his model for the economic crisis. Its main fund, Pure Alpha, has been investing in macro-trends since 1991, making an average of 11.9% a year compared to 9.5% of the S&P 500 stock index.

In 2011 Dalio published a 123 page book called "Principles: Life Work", in which he outlined his personal investment logic and philosophy in over 200 "principles". Also in 2011 he entered the list of Bloomberg Markets as one of the 50 most influential people. In 2012 he appeared in the annual list of Time 100 among the 100 most influential people in the world.

In that period, Dalio also initiated a corporate restructuring while maintaining the position of president and co-CEO. In March 2017 he resigned from the position of co-CEO while maintaining that of president and co-head of investments.

In July 2019 Dalio called for a reform of capitalism by describing wealth inequality as a national emergency.

In November 2019, he published a blog post claiming that excess capital, unfunded social responsibilities and government deficits created a recipe for disaster. Dalio called this a "paradigm shift".

The All Season Portfolio

The first time the profile of the All Seasons Portfolio was drawn up dates back to the interview that Anthony Robbins published in his book "Money: master the game" of 2014, and since then the strategy has had millions of admirers.

Investors from all over the world build their portfolios with the rules of the All Seasons, considered the perfect solution to maximize gains in the upward phase and minimize losses in the downward phase.

But from 2014 to today in the economic and financial world many things have happened that have changed the scenarios in which investments move, so much so that, recently, an information note issued by Ray Dalio himself, suggests modifying part of the All Season strategy to adapt it to current times.

Ray Dalio's critique of the traditional investment method

Ray Dalio's major criticism of the structure of traditional portfolios is that they are based on an erroneous assumption.

This assumption is that stocks and bonds provide the right degree of diversification.

But building a portfolio by including only a balanced mix of stocks and bonds actually ends up disregarding protection expectations, precisely in the most critical phases of the market. In fact, diversification of this type has the ugly flaw of ceasing to work just when things turn for the worst.

Traditional assets collapse in unison to the downside during stock market crashes.

According to Ray Dalio, the traditional balanced portfolio is founded on hope: the hope that stocks and bonds do well and that they don't crash simultaneously.

The principle on which the All Seasons portfolio is based

The All Seasons portfolio is based on the concept of the economic cycle as the driving force behind investment trends.

In an economic cycle there are usually 4 possible scenarios that alternate according to global geopolitical events.

ECONOMIC GROWTH (stock markets rising)	PRICE INCREASE (inflation)
ECONOMIC DECREASE (falling equity markets)	PRICE DECREASE (deflation)

In each of the 4 scenarios, there are investment assets that perform well and other assets that, on the other hand, are destined to suffer.

The All Seasons portfolio is made up of a mix of assets capable of performing well overall in all "4 quadrants" unlike what happens to a traditional balanced portfolio.

The ideal composition of an all Seasons portfolio is based on:

- 40% Long-term US bonds
- 15% US medium-term bonds
- 30% US stocks
- 7.5% Raw materials
- 7.5% Gold

A diversification of this type makes it possible to better manage market scenarios that are not favorable for the traditional balanced portfolio.

Let's see how it works in the 4 phases.
- In phases of economic growth, stocks go up.
- In phases of economic downturn, stocks go down but bonds tend to do well;
- During times of rising prices bonds suffer, but commodities and gold tend to do well;
- During periods of falling prices, commodities and gold suffer but bonds grow.

The percentages have been designed to make the interaction between the various assets effective. Obviously this is a much simplified version of the original Bridgewater portfolio.

The intent is to make it replicable for the public of non-professional investors

The historical returns of the All Seasons portfolio

The average return over the past 50 years has been over 7% per year.

But above all, this type of allocation made it possible to contain the effect of the major stock market crashes. For example, during the great financial crisis of 2008, the All Seasons portfolio closed the year at a more than decent -4% while stock markets plummeted by more than 50%.

The current context, however, has profoundly changed compared to the past: the collapse of bond yields, trade tensions, the pandemic may have changed the "playing field" and, perhaps, even the rules.

The problem of zero bond yields

The effectiveness of the All Seasons portfolio today risks being compromised by the very low level of bond yields. The problem is more evident than ever in the world of government bonds that have rates close to zero almost everywhere.

The All Seasons portfolio provides significant exposure to government bonds due to their protective role during stock market crashes. Investment in government bonds tends to do well when rates set by central banks fall. Conversely, it works very badly when rates go up.

Given that today the downward potential of rates is rather limited and, instead, the upward one has no limits, there are those who start to argue that this asset presents more risks than opportunities. For some time, many experts have firmly argued that government bonds are absolutely useless or even harmful as they are no longer able to offer either yield or diversification to the portfolio.

How to rethink the All Seasons portfolio

First of all, government bonds have been a valid diversification tool for over 50 years, so it would be advisable to use caution and common sense before declaring this long-lasting asset definitively useless.

Ray Dalio's new indications on the All Seasons portfolio

During the month of July, the Bridgewater company published a detailed analysis in which it details how the problem of low yields on bond investments can be overcome.

In a nutshell Ray Dalio provides his solution to the problem by providing several options to implement the portfolio in order to make it "solid" even in the new financial context. Let's take a look at what he suggested.

Inflation-indexed bonds.

The first step that the investor should follow is to integrate the traditional bond component with instruments linked to the rise in interest rates.

This will make it possible to maintain an effective protection function in the downturns of the equity markets.

At the same time, inflation-linked bonds (unlike traditional bonds) have the characteristic of increasing their value when interest rates rise due to inflation.

Monetary and credit systems in the world

Although the United States represents the core of the financial and productive world, for a long time there has been talk of an increasingly "tripolar" world.

Europe and China have assumed an increasingly important role in global growth and in stabilizing its dynamics through their central banks. Therefore, European and Chinese bonds may be able to compete with American ones in providing protection for investment portfolios. In particular, China is one of the few countries still able to offer decidedly attractive interest rates.

This means higher yields for the portfolio and also greater potential for appreciation as Chinese rates could fall by driving up the value of bonds.

De-globalization and diversification

For some time now, trade tensions between the United States and China have outlined a process of repatriation of production chains and defense of national production systems.
The global pandemic has accelerated this process. The global lockdown has highlighted the limits of global supply chains with companies that have seen their factories shut down abroad.

This is why we are witnessing a "repatriation" of global production chains.

This phenomenon will likely lead to greater divergence in the performance of global equity markets. While the last decade has been characterized by the dominance of the US market, de-globalization will have to be taken into account in the future by inserting a mix of geographical exposure that takes into account the "three poles": USA, Europe and China.

Implications for the European investor

We said at the beginning that the All Seasons portfolio is theoretically designed for an American investor and offers investment classes expressed in dollars.

It is essential to consider the effect of the euro/dollar exchange rate which can affect performance even in an important way.

For example, very trivially, those who bought dollars at the end of March 2021 would have reported a loss of 12% due to the exchange rate effect.

Obviously this "risk" also represents an opportunity for gain when the dollar appreciates against the euro.

Exchange rate fluctuations can compromise portfolio performance

This risk can be managed by using investment products hedged against exchange rate risk. In this way, the effect of the oscillation between the euro and the dollar is neutralized. However, it must be considered that this coverage has a cost that fluctuates over time according to different financial conditions.

The most logical solution is to use it moderately and intelligently.

If you are buying single stocks as an European investor, we advise you to choose companies listed on European exchanges. If you are investing in ETFs for the long term, you can decide not to consider the exchange ratio, as both proved to be among the most resilient currencies out there.

Chapter 16

The Investing Philosophy of Bill Ackman

Activist investor William "Bill" Ackman heads Pershing Square Capital Management and is one of the best-known investors in Wall Street circles. He is known for his strong bearish stance on Herbalife Ltd., a move that sparked a series of confrontations between Ackman and other investment titans such as Carl Icahn and Daniel Loeb.

On the market, Ackman is known for being very hungry for victory and for his high self-esteem.

Ackman and the Herbalife case

Ackman first opened a $1 billion short position against the dietary supplement company five years ago, accusing the organization of following a pyramid scheme. The decision brought him into stark opposition to investor Carl Icahn, who became Herbalife's largest shareholder as Ackman waged his campaign against the company.

But instead of going down, Herbalife's stock has been up 95% since Ackman first publicly revealed that he was betting against the company. Later, in November 2017, Ackman revealed that he was less sure of his position on Herbalife. The billionaire converted the short position, which in theory could lead to considerable losses for Ackman, into put options. At the end of February 2018, it was announced that Ackman had permanently eliminated his bet against Herbalife.

The decision came after Pershing Squares posted its third consecutive year of negative returns in 2017 due to a series of bets. For example, Ackman abandoned his stake in the pharmaceutical company Valeant in early 2017, causing losses of billions to its shareholders. Meanwhile, the fund has cut nearly 20% of staff in an attempt to return the hedge fund to its glory days.

Private life and education

Growing up in Chappaqua, New York, in a wealthy Jewish family, Bill Ackman enjoyed many advantages in life. He took advantage of all his opportunities he was given by studying hard as a child and earning a reputation as the one who knew everything.

Ackman graduated with honors from Harvard University in 1988 with a degree in history. Four years later he earned his Master of Business Administration from Harvard Business School. Later, Ackman joined the Board of Dean's Advisors at Harvard Business School.

The story of a successful investor

Shortly after his graduation from Harvard Business School, Ackman founded Gotham Partners with David P. Berkowitz. Gotham Partners was a small investment firm specializing in a diversified portfolio of public companies, a style far away from current Ackman's investment strategies. Despite years of success in the initial phase, the fund closed in 2002 after a decade of activity, largely due to poor feedback from some investments in golf courses and the relentlessness of some outside investors.

Two years after the liquidation of Gotham Partners, Ackman founded Pershing Square Capital Management with $54 million from his personal funds. In the decade that followed, Pershing Square has earned a reputation as a brutally effective negotiator capable of fueling business change, gaining significant influence among major corporations such as JC Penney Company, General Growth Properties, Fortune Brands, Kraft Foods and others.

Heritage and philanthropy

As of Mya, 2021, Bill Ackman has a net worth of $3 billion. Most of Bill Ackman's professional income comes from the market as a portfolio manager, although he also worked with his father in real estate for a few years. In addition to being a well-known investor, Bill Ackman is also a philanthropist.

With his wife Karen, Ackman founded The Pershing Square Foundation in 2006 to support education, health care, human rights and the arts. The foundation has granted and invested over $160 million in charitable initiatives between 2006 and 2015.

His courage and self trust are what makes him a great investor. We highly encourage you to take a closer look at his life. We are sure you are going to find some pretty interesting tips to master the art of investing.

Chapter 17

Short Selling

In a previous chapter we have seen how Bill Ackman is incredibly good at betting against companies. This practice is called short selling and in this chapter we tell you more about it.

Short selling is a financial transaction that consists in the sale of unowned financial instruments with subsequent repurchase. This operation is carried out if it is believed that the price at which the financial instruments will be repurchased will be lower than the price initially collected through the sale.

If that would be the case, the overall return of the transaction would be positive; on the contrary, it would be negative if the price of the instrument increases.

How short selling works

In detail, the financial instruments subject to short selling are temporarily lent to the short seller by the bank or by a financial intermediary.

Usually, for the aforementioned loan, an interest is paid to the broker in relation to the duration in days of the short sale operation. In addition to claiming the established annual interest (which may also vary based on the individual security), the broker requires a guarantee margin for the operation (for example 50% of the exchange value).

The logic behind a short sale operation is reversed compared to that of a normal operation, which first involves the purchase and then the sale of the instrument and which can therefore be used in phases of market descent.

What are the limitations of a short sale

In the case of a short sale, the potential profit is limited compared to a normal purchase operation with subsequent sale. In fact, if there is no upper limit to the appreciation of the value of a financial instrument, there is a lower limit of zero. At the same time, by virtue of this consideration, the potential loss is unlimited for the short seller. This is the reason why, as mentioned above, the broker not only freezes the funds from the short sale, as a guarantee and coverage of the subsequent repurchase, but also requires an additional amount (the guarantee margin). This is done to protect the broker from the possibility that the seller is able to cover themselves by repurchasing the aforementioned financial instruments with prices considerably higher than those of sale.

The broker releases the margin at the same time as the position is closed, or when the financial instruments are repurchased. This operation is technically referred to as overdraft coverage.

A practical example

Suppose an investor believes that the ABC stock is experiencing a bearish price movement. They may decide to sell this stock even if they do not own it. For example, they decide to sell 1000 X shares at the current price of 10 dollars. Having verified the availability of the broker to lend the quantity of security X being sold, the investor sells and collects the equivalent, equal to 10,000 dollars. The broker freezes what the investor has collected from the sale plus an additional amount called the guarantee margin. Let's assume 50%, therefore 5,000 dollars. If the transaction is not closed on the same day, the broker will require the investor to pay interest on the value of the transaction, let's assume equal to 20% on an annual basis. The amount of interest will depend on the duration of the transaction. Assuming that this is 5 days, the interest to be paid will be equal to ($10,000 x 20 x 5) / 36500, ie $27.7.

Let's assume that, after 5 days, on the closing date of the transaction, the forecasts turned out to be correct and the price of the stock fell to 9 dollars. The investor will be able to buy back 1000 shares at the price of 9 dollars by spending 9,000 and return them to the broker who had lent them to them. The total profit realized will be equal to 972.3 dollars(i.e. 10,000 - 9,000 - 27.7).

As you can see, short selling can be risky as your losses can exceed your initial investment. We only recommend buying shares in the classical way if you are a beginner. Learn from gurus, do not imitate what they do if you are not able to replicate it.

Conclusion

Congratulations on making it to the end of this book, we hope you found some useful insights to take your stock investing skills to the next level. As you should know by now, the world of stocks is extremely complicated and there is a new "opportunity" every way you look. However, our experience tells us that only by taking things seriously and having a proper plan you can develop your investing skills to the point that you can actually accumulate wealth.

Our final advice is to stay away from the shining objects that the world of stocks offers you every day. Simply dollar cost average into a broad ETF and study the world of stocks in depth. After you have sufficient knowledge on what you are talking about, you can go ahead and invest into single companies. Analyze your results, improve your money management skills and become the master of your emotions.

As you can see, there are no shortcuts you can take. Easy money does not exist. What exists is the possibility to start from zero and work your way up to become a professional stock investor. The journey might be difficult, but it is certainly worth it.